# Theory Workbook

Grade **7**

Written by
Anthony Crossland &
Terence Greaves

**ABRSM**

First published in 1999 by ABRSM (Publishing) Ltd,
a wholly owned subsidiary of ABRSM

Reprinted in 2019

© 1999 by The Associated Board of the Royal Schools of Music

AB 2717

A CIP catalogue record for this book is available from The British Library.

Extracts from the following copyright works are reproduced with permission:

R. Strauss: *Burleske* for piano and orchestra
Vaughan Williams: *Serenade to Music*

Typeset by Musonix
Printed in England by Halstan & Co. Ltd, Amersham, Bucks.,
on materials from sustainable sources

# Contents

The system of chord labelling used in this workbook is 'extended Roman'. It best identifies the sound quality of the chord and its function within the key. Please note, however, that examination candidates may use any recognised method of chord labelling, provided it presents a clear indication or a precise description of the harmony.

# Introduction

This *Theory Workbook* provides straightforward information and advice about, and practice for, the Associated Board's Grade 7 theory exam papers. It focuses on the skills, knowledge and understanding that are being tested at the grade, exploring each specific element of the syllabus in some detail and providing insights into how candidates can approach their papers in a positive frame of mind and with every chance of success.

The workbook is complementary to the Board's range of related theory publications, in particular *The AB Guide to Music Theory* and *Harmony in Practice*. With all these, students will be supremely well-equipped to acquire the essential theory skills and understanding they need for their musical development in general and undertaking their Associated Board Grade 7 Theory exam in particular.

**Philip Mundey**
**Director of Examinations**

# Question 1

In this question two staves of music are given: a bass line, or 'basso continuo', with a solo line above it. At the opening, figures are inserted below the bass line which indicate the implied harmony above, and you are asked to continue this figuring to the end. To help you, asterisks are placed under the notes where figures are required, together with horizontal lines which indicate the continuation of the previous harmony. (For figured bass see *The AB Guide to Music Theory*, Part I 8/4 and *Harmony in Practice*, 'Chord Labelling'.)

The passage will be in a major or minor key which is unlikely to exceed four sharps or four flats. Its melodic line is likely to fall within one of two stylistic categories:

1. A flowing melody which contains decoration in the form of passing notes, auxiliary notes, suspensions, and so on. (For an introduction to melodic decoration see *The AB Guide to Music Theory*, Part II Chapter 15, and for further comment see *Harmony in Practice*, Chapters 5 and 14.)

2. A more steadily moving melody with fewer decorations but involving chromatic alteration (particularly if the piece is in a minor key), which will require special care when figuring is inserted.

An example of both types of melody is given here, followed by step-by-step procedures for working the question. Each is preceded by an introductory paragraph such as you will find in the exam paper itself.

## Sample Question 1

This was used in the 1998C Grade 7 exam paper and is taken from J. S. Bach's Cantata 'Wachet auf, ruft uns die Stimme'. It has a steadily moving bass line with more rapidly flowing semiquavers above, which contain a considerable amount of melodic decoration.

**Indicate suitable chords for a continuo player by figuring the bass as necessary, *from bar 2*, at the places marked \* in this passage. If you wish to use a $\frac{5}{3}$ chord, leave the space under the asterisk blank, but $\frac{5}{3}$ chords *must* be shown as part of a $\frac{6\ 5}{4\ 3}$ progression or when chromatic alteration is required. All other chords should be indicated, as should any suspended dissonances.**

2

etc.

Before beginning to work the question you should fix clearly in your mind what is required. The asterisks show where chords are to be indicated (and note particularly what the question says about the $\frac{5}{3}$ chord) and continuation lines show that the harmony implied by the preceding figure lasts for the duration of the line. Thus in bar 1 the 6 _____ means a B♭ chord in first inversion, then in root position on the next quaver beat and back to first inversion on the following quaver.

If you feel that an asterisk followed by a continuation line requires a straightforward $\frac{5}{3}$ chord then leave the space below it blank. For example, in bar 2 third to fourth crotchet beat where (as we shall see) a $\frac{5}{3}$ is the best option, no chord indication is needed in the completed working. But as you come to such places in your working it is advisable to put a light pencil dot under the asterisk to remind yourself that it has been dealt with.

### WORKING THE QUESTION

Now begin with two essential first steps:

1.  Look through the whole passage to establish and absorb thoroughly its key. This example is in the key of B♭ major, and it is a good idea to write this lightly in pencil at the beginning as a reminder.

2.  Decide where the main phrases start and finish, and note the implied cadences at these points. In this example it should be fairly clear that there are three phrases with associated cadences:

    **(a)**  halfway through bar 2 – perfect cadence in the tonic key (B♭ major).
    **(b)**  halfway through bar 4 – imperfect cadence in the tonic key.
    **(c)**  halfway through bar 6 – imperfect cadence in the tonic key.

In fixing these important landmarks for your working of this type of question it is usually best to look primarily at the bass line. Melodic decoration, which may occur frequently in the upper part, can cause considerable confusion as to what are harmony notes and what are not – accented or unaccented passing notes, auxiliary notes, appoggiaturas, and so on.

As well as indicating the cadences, the bass line will give you a much clearer picture of what is happening to the harmony, and once the chord patterns are broadly established, you will find that much of the task of deciding which are harmony and which are non-harmony notes in the upper part has been done for you.

Let us now return to our working and pencil in the phrases and cadence points, at which the relevant chords may be decided as follows:

**Bar 2**    The perfect cadence will be formed by a $V^7$ chord on the fourth bass quaver (this is automatically shown by the compound 7th interval between bass and melody notes), preceded either by a Ic or a Va chord, the former perhaps having greater harmonic interest. The crotchet appoggiatura is an ornamental addition and it does not, of course, affect the harmonic structure of the cadence.

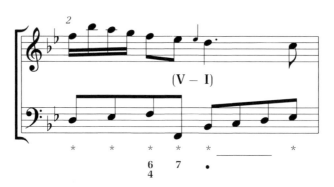

> ✳ *Mention was made in the above paragraph of a chord being automatically shown by the harmonic interval between the given bass and melody notes. This is sometimes the case, but not exclusively so, and many candidates make the serious mistake of deciding on the figuring solely by using this method. **Harmonic intervals should only be used for chord identification in conjunction with other evidence.***

**Bar 4**    Here the tonic–dominant harmony is simply achieved, with a chord of Ia on the fourth bass quaver, followed by Va. The approach chord for this cadence, on the third bass quaver, is most satisfactorily a $\frac{6}{5}$ chord, creating a smoother progression than the use of the more angular $\frac{5}{3}$ diminished triad on the bass note A which is suggested by the interval between the two given notes.

This matter of achieving a smooth harmonic progression is important, and to demonstrate we will anticipate slightly and consider the first crotchet beat of bar 4. One chord is implied here – the chord of B♭ (the E♭ semiquaver in the upper part being an accented passing note). Reducing the essential harmony of the half-bar on to a single stave shows this smooth, conjunct movement, and playing it will confirm the satisfactory musical result:

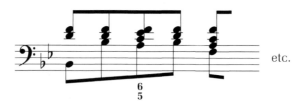

**Bar 6**   Though the bass has a quaver rest on the third beat of the bar, dominant harmony is plainly implied at the next quaver beat. The asterisk and line indicate the use of one chord on the second crotchet beat, and a look at the bass notes (E♭ and C) together with essential harmony notes in the melody (G and B♭) point to a 7th chord, which is shown by ⁶₅ figuring under the bass E♭. This gives a standard ii–V imperfect cadence progression. The supertonic harmony is reinforced by the use of a straightforward C minor chord for the first beat of the bar.

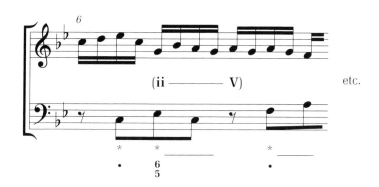

At this stage in our working, the passage should look like this:

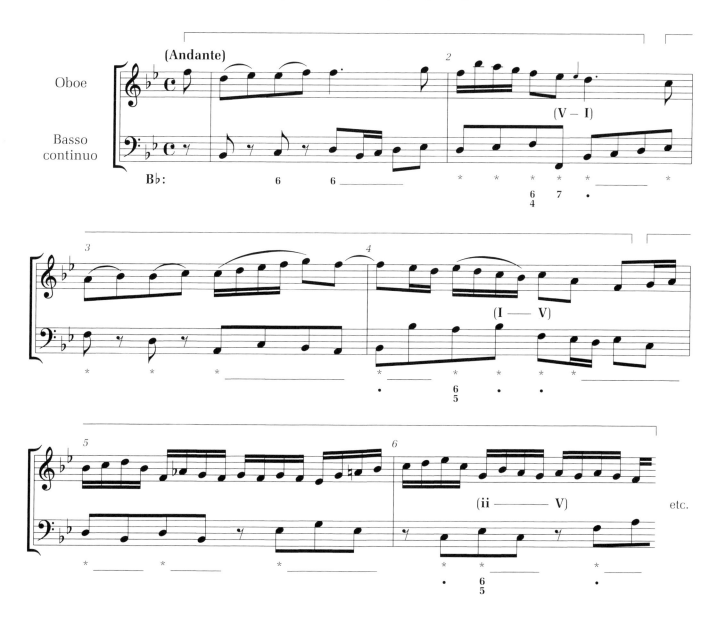

*It is essential that you begin your working of this question by following the steps discussed above, which are:*

1.  **Identify and mark in the phrase structure.**

2.  **Figure the cadence and approach chord(s) at the end of each phrase.** (See *Harmony in Practice*, Chapter 9 'Approaching the cadence'.)

*Though this process may seem lengthy, you will find that, in the long run, it is quicker and much more reliable than working straight through, chord by chord, from the beginning to the end: a method that lacks organisation and which can so easily lead to confusion and error.*

Having established these key points of the harmonic structure, it now remains to fill in the gaps. First, look through the passage for two particular features:

1.  Any accidentals which might indicate a modulation. These may occur either at cadences or (as we shall see here) within a phrase.

2.  Any points of melodic imitation or repetition which give immediate clues to the underlying harmony.

Examples of both of the above appear in the third phrase of the melody, and so we will consider this section now. First, the melodic line only:

1.  The introduction of an A♭ implies a transient modulation to the sub-dominant key of E♭ major, which is cancelled by the A♮ later in the bar.

2.  The melodic line of the first bar of the phrase is repeated sequentially one tone higher in the next bar.

Now the harmonic structure of the whole phrase:

The first bar of the phrase (bar 5) should immediately suggest B♭ major moving to E♭ major by way of the dominant 7th chord in the key of E♭. The sequential character of the next bar will then automatically give the harmony as C minor (because of the E♭ in the key signature) moving to F major – also by way of a 7th, this time a supertonic 7th in the tonic key of B♭. (See how the chord pattern in bar 5 (B♭$^7$ rising a 4th to E♭) is echoed a tone higher in bar 6 (Cm$^7$ rising a 4th to F), matching the sequence in the melody.) You will notice that this confirms the harmony for bar 6 which had already been arrived at earlier in the working of the question.

Here is the third phrase with the figuring in place:

etc.

It now remains to go back and supply the figuring for the first two phrases:

**Phrase 1**   Two chords have to be decided here, for the first two quavers of bar 2. The first is given automatically by the two semiquavers in the upper part: the leap from F to the unaccented B♭ indicates that they are both harmony notes and they produce a first inversion chord above the bass D. The second chord links this first inversion of B♭ with the second inversion already fixed on the third quaver beat. Theoretically either a first inversion or root position chord would be possible above the bass E♭ but in order to maintain a smooth harmonic flow a root position chord is preferable as it has a B♭ in common with the preceding and following chords.

**Phrase 2**   The interval of a 6th between the bass and melody notes in the first chord of the phrase (the last quaver beat of bar 2) suggests a $\frac{6}{3}$ chord, as do the given notes on the second beat of bar 3, and these can be smoothly linked by a root position chord on the first beat of bar 3. One chord only is specified for the second half of bar 3, and the broad harmonic implication is clearly dominant, followed by tonic at the beginning of bar 4. A simple $\frac{6}{3}$ chord might be possible for the second half of bar 3, but experiment will show that incorporation of the third semiquaver E♭ melody note to give a $\frac{6}{5}$ chord will produce a richer sound. It might be thought that separate harmony should be used for the first quaver of the fourth beat, but the continuation line shows that this is not the case. The apparently alien notes are absorbed by the $\frac{6}{5}$ harmony and may be explained as an accented passing note B♭ in the bass and an appoggiatura melody G.

There is now only one more chord to supply – the connecting chord between phrases 2 and 3.

The harmonic movement here is from dominant (end of phrase 2) to tonic (beginning of bar 5), and the two E♭ bass notes suggest a change of the F major chord into a dominant 7th (in third inversion) which links smoothly and naturally with the following B♭ harmony.

Here is the completed working, with these final additions in place and phrase marks and other incidental markings removed. It is a good idea, if you have time, to rub out such markings in your working, but you will not be penalised if you leave them in.

# Sample Question 2

This is adapted from a Partita for violin and basso continuo by Georg Philipp Telemann. It contains fewer examples of melodic decoration, but will require careful thought as far as chromatic alteration is concerned, this aspect being heightened by the fact that the extract is in a minor key.

**Indicate suitable chords for a continuo player by figuring the bass as necessary, *from the second beat of bar 3*, at the places marked * in this passage. If you wish to use a $\frac{5}{3}$ chord, leave the space under the asterisk blank, but $\frac{5}{3}$ chords *must* be shown as part of a $\frac{6}{4}\frac{5}{3}$ progression or when chromatic alteration is required. All other chords should be indicated, as should any suspended dissonances.**

### WORKING THE QUESTION

The first step, as in Sample Question 1, is to establish the key and phrase/cadence structure.

1.   You will see that the key at the start is G minor, and this should be pencilled in at the beginning, as a reminder. (See *Harmony in Practice*, page 5 and Chapter 11 'Scale movement in a minor key'.)

2.   The phrase structure of the melodic line is by no means as balanced and clear-cut as in the first sample question. If this problem arises, look instead at the bass line, remembering that we are not interested in phrase structure as such, but only in any indications which it might give to modulations or harmonic direction.

Here the first four bars of the bass line imply G minor harmony at the beginning and end, with a perfect cadence from bar 3 to bar 4, which calls for just two root position chords – dominant (D major) and tonic (G minor). Remember, though, that the dominant chord in a minor key usually has a sharpened 3rd, and so a ♯ sign is necessary below the D in bar 3.

   *Omitting to indicate such sharpened 3rds in minor key questions (F♯ here and B♮ in bar 8 for the dominant of C minor) is probably the most common single error made by candidates in the exam.*

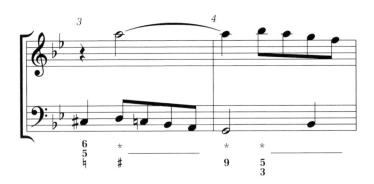

The tied A in the melody at the beginning of bar 4 may look puzzling at first glance, but you will see that the bass notes of the bar clearly call for G minor harmony, and this is confirmed by the descending quaver figure of the melody. The A thus becomes a suspension with decorative resolution, and should be figured with a 9 under the first beat of the bar, and a $\frac{5}{3}$ under the second beat. The normal figuring for this suspension would be 9–8: the 9–$\frac{5}{3}$ figuring is used here to make clear what is intended in view of the unusual upward resolution of the suspended 9th.

Now look at the bass line of the second, five-bar, phrase and you will see a shift to C minor, plainly identified by a perfect cadence in that key at bars 8–9. Notice also that C minor harmony is implied at the beginning of bar 8, as an approach chord to the cadence, and that it is also implied in bar 6.

These features may now be put in, with pencilled cadences and permanent indications, as necessary, for the chords involved. The passage will look like this:

Let us now look at bars 5 and 6. We have already noted that the last chord of bar 6 is C minor and it will probably be simplest to work back from this.

---

✳ *Quite frequently you may find it quicker and more straightforward to work backwards from a cadence or other established point, rather than working exclusively from the beginning.*

---

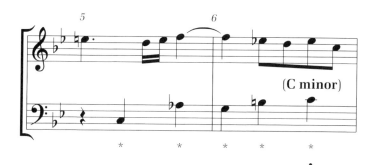

The B♮ on the second beat of bar 6 strongly suggests a dominant chord in C minor, and this will work perfectly well if we regard the E♭ above as an accented passing note, and the D as the note essential to the harmony, thus giving a simple ⁶₃ chord. The first chord of the bar then becomes a dominant 7th in C minor, with the melody note suspended from the previous bar. (Remember when figuring this that a natural sign for the 3rd will be needed in addition to the 7th figuring.)

Moving back to bar 5, the interval of a compound 6th between bass and melody on the last beat indicates a ⁶₃ chord. The bass C which precedes this has to take into account the E♮ melody note which begins the bar, and this means a straightforward ⁵₃ or 7th chord. Either would be musically sound, but again remember to indicate the natural 3rd in your figuring.

This is the completed version of these two bars, in which a simple ⁵₃ chord has been chosen for the beginning of bar 5:

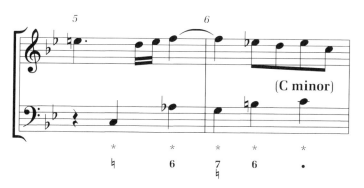

It now remains to complete the last three bars of the passage which, at the moment, look like this:

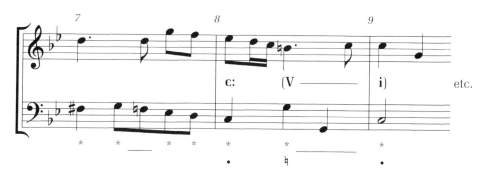

The final cadence has already been fixed, as has the use of a C minor chord for the beginning of bar 8. The last two quavers of bar 7 need two separate chords and, at first glance, the number of possibilities for these might seem confusing. We will therefore turn our attention to the first two beats of the bar, in the hope that a decision about these chords will help to guide our thinking for the last two chords of the bar.

The first two bass notes, F♯ and G, in conjunction with the held D in the top line, might suggest a perfect cadence in our home key of G minor. This is a possibility but, bearing in mind the C minor harmony already established at the end of bar 6 and in bar 8, it is preferable to keep our sense of harmonic direction more firmly fixed around this key centre. We can do this quite easily by making the first chord of bar 7 D major in first inversion (turning it into a $\frac{6}{5}$ 7th chord will give a richer sound) and follow this with a chord of G major, which serves neatly as a dominant chord in C minor. The last two quaver chords of bar 7 then fall into place as C minor first inversion, followed by a leading-note chord in C minor, also in first inversion. Remember to insert a ♮ sign in the figuring of the latter.

Figuring for these chords may now be inserted (remember all the accidentals needed!) and the final working, with the various pencilled reminders removed, will look like this:

▶   **CHECKLIST OF PROCEDURES FOR WORKING THIS QUESTION**

1. Establish the key of the passage.

2. Establish the phrase structure from either the melodic or bass line.

3. Identify and figure the main cadences and, if possible, the approach chords.

4. Identify and figure the remainder of the chords, dividing the music into short sections. To help you do this, remember to:

- Look out for accidentals in the given parts which may give clues to modulation or harmonic direction.

- Look out for any sequences or repeated passages.

- Note the intervals between bass and melody notes which may help to suggest implied harmony.

- Mark in all accidentals that are required in chords, even when they appear in the melody line.

- Use the option of working backwards from a fixed point (usually a cadence).

- Mark lightly in pencil all unfigured $\frac{5}{3}$ chords so that you do not overlook any of the asterisks.

# Question 1   Sample Questions

In the following sample questions, 1 to 6 are more simple in character and contain a smaller range of chord choices. Sample questions 7 to 12 may require the use of any of the chords specified for Grade 7, and represent the standard of the questions set for the exam.

**Indicate suitable chords for a continuo player by figuring the bass as necessary at the places marked * in the following passages. If you wish to use a $\frac{5}{3}$ chord, leave the space under the asterisk blank, but $\frac{5}{3}$ chords *must* be shown as part of a $\frac{6\ 5}{4\ 3}$ progression or when chromatic alteration is required. All other chords should be indicated, as should any suspended dissonances.**

The starting point for your working is given before each individual exercise.

1.   Begin to indicate chords from the beginning of bar 3. Only $\frac{5}{3}$ and $\frac{6}{3}$ chords are used in this passage, apart from one $\frac{6}{4}$ chord in the approach to the final cadence.

2.  Begin to indicate chords from the beginning of bar 3. Only $\frac{5}{3}$, $\frac{6}{3}$ and $\frac{6}{4}$ chords are needed. However, remember that accidentals (even in $\frac{5}{3}$ chords) must be shown in the figuring, and these are always likely to be needed in minor keys, such as the passage in bars 3–4.

Loeillet: Oboe sonata (adapted)

3.  Indicate chords from the beginning of bar 3. It is possible to make a satisfactory working by using just $\frac{5}{3}$ and $\frac{6}{3}$ chords, but Handel did include in this passage three 7th chords (including the one in bar 2) and one 4–3 progression. You might like to work the question in the simple way first, and then try to find the places where these more adventurous features were used.

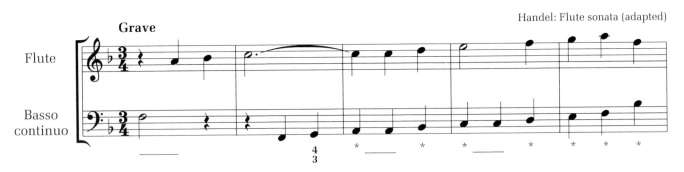

Handel: Flute sonata (adapted)

etc.

**4.** Indicate chords from the beginning of bar 3. Only $\frac{5}{3}$, $\frac{6}{3}$ and one $\frac{6}{4}$ chord are needed. Treat the first quaver of the last beats of bars 4 and 5 (marked with †) as accented passing notes. The penultimate B♭ in the violin part (marked ‡) is a note of anticipation and does not affect the harmony. Similar examples of this will be found in questions 5, 7, 8, 9 and 10.

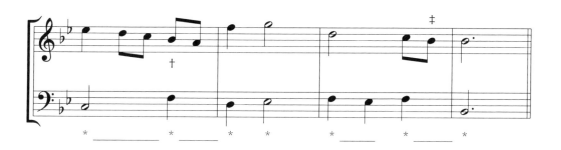

**5.** Indicate chords from the beginning of bar 3. Only $\frac{5}{3}$ and $\frac{6}{3}$ chords are needed, but remember that all accidentals that are to be used within chords in this minor key example must be shown.

**6.** Indicate chords from the beginning of bar 3. This exercise is generally straightforward but one 7th chord is needed.

**7.** Indicate chords from the beginning of bar 5.

**8.**   Indicate chords from the beginning of bar 5.

**9.**   Indicate chords from the beginning of bar 4.

etc.

**10.** Indicate chords from the beginning of bar 5. Note that the music moves into A minor at bar 7, and treat the first semiquaver of the last beat of bar 8 (marked †) as an accented passing note.

etc.

**11.** Indicate chords from the beginning of bar 4.

etc.

**12.** Indicate chords from the beginning of bar 4. Note the modulations to G major, D major and A minor, which will affect your chord choices, and remember to show the suspensions and resolutions in bar 8 in your figuring.

Tartini: Violin sonata

etc.

# Question 2

In this question you are given two sets of staves, marked **A** and **B** respectively. Staves **A** contain the harmonic skeleton of a short passage of music, whilst staves **B** give the opening bars as the composer wrote them, and may also contain further fragments of the original music. Your task is to complete staves **B** in the style of this given material, adding various notes of decoration, suspensions, and so on to the harmonic outline provided by staves **A**.

The opening of staves **B** will give you a broad indication of the expected style, whilst any later fragments may provide valuable clues to what is required in that particular area of the extract, and all this material should be studied carefully before you begin to work the question.

We shall consider two stylistically different examples for this question. The first is a chorale by J. S. Bach. Note that while this type of extract appears quite frequently in exams, it is not the only type that you may encounter. The syllabus is not specific about a particular historical period and candidates should be prepared to deal with other composers and musical styles. Our second example, therefore, is taken from a piano sonata by Haydn, and will provide a contrast both of style and musical medium – four-part voices in the former, and keyboard in the latter.

Whatever the period or composer, no great compositional skills will be necessary to produce a good answer. The question merely seeks an ability to continue and develop the given material in a way which is faithful to its style and correct in musical grammar.

## Sample Question 1

**On the staves marked A below is an outline of a chorale harmonisation, 'Nun komm, der Heiden Heiland', by J. S. Bach, leaving out certain suspensions, passing notes and other notes of melodic decoration. The music on the staves marked B is what the composer actually wrote. Continuing in the same style, reconstruct the partially completed bars.**

As a general preparation to working a chorale question you are strongly advised to study and play as many of Bach's chorale harmonisations as you can. A number of them may be found in the standard hymn-books, but the great collection made by Albert Riemenschneider, which is available in print (Schirmer, 1941), will provide the richest source.

You will find that careful consideration of these provides invaluable insights into Bach's style and 'tricks of the trade'; it will soon become evident that the fundamental aim of his decoration of the various vocal parts is to give each individual line as much melodic interest as possible. In this way the chorale, instead of being a potentially dull succession of four-part chords, becomes four melodies combining to form a harmonious whole, and in your working of this question you should always be aware of the horizontal shape and direction of each vocal part.

To achieve this shape and interest Bach makes use of the following main devices:

- Passing notes, either accented or unaccented.

- Auxiliary notes.

- Suspensions.

- Tied notes (sometimes combined with passing notes).

- Leaps to another harmony note of the same chord.

The above should form your basic armoury for working the question and, as we shall see, they all figure at some point in our present example, to which we now return.

Before beginning the working, have the following points clear in your mind:

- The pause marks do not necessarily imply pauses as such, but indicate the ends of lines of the sung text, and form a vocal equivalent to the ends of phrases in instrumental music. An important practical point associated with this is that Bach virtually never linked chorale phrases by embellishment of the final notes of a phrase. Very occasionally a suspension might be used at this point, for example, causing the first phrase of our chorale to end as shown left, but such instances are very rare and it is probably safest to stick to a general rule of allowing all final chords in each phrase to be undecorated.

- In this particular example the top vocal line is given throughout. In examples where this is not the case, very little embellishment should be used in the top part. As it provides the melody of the hymn the normal practice is to keep it as straightforward as possible, and an occasional passing note where appropriate is usually all that is likely to be required, as will be seen here.

- Make sure that a lower part does not go above the soprano melodic line. This does occur in Bach's writing, but only very occasionally, and in student workings it is best avoided.

- Take care that any additions or alterations which you make do not conflict with the given harmonic skeleton and do not cause errors of musical grammar. The addition of passing notes, for example, can easily produce consecutive 5ths or octaves, and you should check your working constantly for faults of this kind.

- Remember that it is not essential to embellish every beat of every bar. Your working can be as easily marred by too much adornment as by too little.

- As your working progresses, **play it at regular intervals, as this will help you acquire the ability to hear in your head what you have written**.

## WORKING THE QUESTION

When beginning the working, as always, a systematic approach should be adopted. All too frequently exam papers look as though decorative features have been scattered haphazardly, when just a small degree of thought and planning would take very little more time and would produce a much more satisfactory musical result.

In Question 1, you will remember, we added a harmonic framework and the recommendation was to fix cadences and phrases first. Here the cadences and harmonic framework are already in place and your task is to produce pleasing melodic lines. This means thinking horizontally and the best way to work this question is to **add each line, individually, phrase by phrase**. If you attempt to deal with all the parts at once, not only are grammatical errors more likely to creep in, but you are much more likely to lose sight of the basic need for shape and interest in each of the vocal lines.

We begin by completing the bass line. A strong and convincing foundation to the piece is vital, and once this is in place the inner parts should not present too many difficulties. Any or all of our five main embellishment devices may be used in the bass line but remember that, as it is less subject to restrictions of spacing than the inner parts, the bass line is particularly suitable for the addition of jumps to other harmony notes in the same chord (see the end of the first bar of stave **B**). Also, if two successive bass notes are the same, greater melodic interest can be gained by using an auxiliary note between them or by raising the second note an octave rather than repeating the same pitch. (See the beginning of bar 3, where the octave leap gives strength to the line and also provides an easier melodic approach to the succeeding note A.)

Let us now work through the remainder of the bass part, phrase by phrase.

**Phrase 2**     The only obvious opportunity here is for a passing note G to be inserted after the third crotchet note of bar 3:

**Phrase 3**   Here, too, is the chance to put in a passing note between the last note of bar 5 and the first note of bar 6:

In view of the sparse decoration used in phrase 2 a little more movement would be desirable here in phrase 3, so we might look for further possibilities. One such would be to link the last two crotchets of bar 5 with two semiquavers – a passing note E and a harmony note F♯. This would give a perfectly satisfactory musical result and is a device quite often used by Bach (as here, in the alto part at the end of bar 1). A possible reason that he did not use it on this occasion is given on page 28, but this merely highlights the fact that there is not just one 'correct' working for this question. Various options are usually open to you, and as long as your working meets the two requirements of stylistic suitability and correctness of musical grammar, it does not have to be a note-by-note recreation of what Bach actually wrote. He himself often composed more than one harmonisation of the same chorale melody.

What Bach did at bar 5 was to decorate the first two crotchets, like this:

As you will see, this is a clever combination of an unaccented passing note E with an accented passing note D – a characteristic trick of Bach's which is well worth remembering.

**Phrase 4**   Passing notes may be put in to join the first two notes of bar 7, and the last note of bar 7 with the first of bar 8:

The two F♯s at the end of bar 7 also offer scope for decoration along the lines mentioned above concerning repeated bass notes. An octave leap would clearly not work here but a lower auxiliary note E (or E♯) would add interest and make an effective start to the rising quaver melodic figure.

The bass line is now complete and is given below. It remains to check the line carefully with the soprano part to make sure there are no consecutives.

We will now turn to the tenor part. The same phrase-by-phrase procedure will be followed but as the number of parts in your working increases you should give equally increasing attention to the vertical texture which is emerging. The overall aim is to give the individual parts melodic interest and also to see that the vertical harmonic progression of crotchet chords is broken up by shorter note values in one part or another. This should not be taken to imply that every single crotchet chord has to be joined to its neighbours by decorative quavers. The musical strength of such a progression as the following, particularly at the beginning of a piece or phrase, is immediately apparent:

J. S. Bach, Chorale: 'Christus, der ist mein Leben'

and Bach might easily have begun our example as follows, with good musical effect:

Too many block chords, however, can become monotonous, and a balanced texture with a reasonable degree of flowing movement, but which is not over-fussy with excessive detail, should be your aim. Be sure also not to use a succession of very short-value notes. If the chorale has a crotchet pulse (which is the norm), groups of four semiquavers should not be written. Bach frequently used rhythmic groups of quaver plus two semiquavers, or vice versa, but not normally blocks of four semiquavers. Similarly, never write any instrumental ornamentation, such as mordents or turns, in chorale workings as these are alien to this particular style.

With these points in mind we will now proceed to complete the tenor part.

**Phrase 2**    Very little has to be done here. A passing note C♯ between the first two notes of bar 3 suggests itself, and that is all:

Bach's harmony for bar 4, which is given in full, contains two interesting features.

First, the spacing between tenor and alto parts in the first two beats: Bach's wish to give the tenor and alto lines melodic interest leads him to break the rule which says that a gap of more than an octave should only exist between bass and tenor, and you might feel tempted to adjust the inner notes of the harmonic skeleton on staves **A** to give better spacing here. But remember that **all the notes of each main beat in the harmonic outline are essential for the working on staves B**, either as harmony notes or notes of melodic decoration, and none should be disregarded.

Secondly, the tenor figure used on the second beat of the bar is important. It is a device frequently used by Bach at a perfect cadence (this may be regarded as a perfect cadence in G) when the supertonic rises in the same part to the mediant. The mediant is anticipated and followed by an upper auxiliary note on the subdominant (C♮ in this example), the auxiliary note forming a passing 7th above the bass:

It is useful to remember this characteristic of Bach's style which may be used in two different rhythmic groupings: either ♩♬ as here, or ♬♩ as in the tenor part of the last bar.

**Phrase 3**   In bar 5 a passing note may be put in to join the notes D and B of the third and fourth beats:

In bar 6 you will see that there are already two quavers in the soprano part between the first and second beats. Bach generally maintains rhythmic momentum right up to the last note of a phrase, so it would be desirable to continue this movement between the second and third beats. Looking ahead, it should be noted that the alto will not be able to take a passing note here since, when the leading note falls to the dominant at a cadence, Bach never fills in the interval with a passing note (see page 28). In any case, such a passing note would require a G♯ (to follow on melodically from the A♯) and that would produce an unpleasant tritone effect with the following tenor D. Therefore we should consider introducing movement in the tenor part, and three options are available:

1.   Use of the figure in the tenor part of bar 4.

2.   A leap to another harmony note, using two quavers – C♯ and F♯.

3.   Use of the C♯–F♯ leap but adding an E passing note.

These possibilities look like this:

All are possible but as the first option has already appeared in bar 4 of the tenor part it might be rather monotonous to use it again here. Either of the other two is equally effective.

**Phrase 4**   Bar 7 already contains generous movement in the bass. In the tenor we see the chance to add an accented passing note C♯ on the second beat:

The tenor part is then complete. Check it, first with the bass, and then with the soprano line for consecutives before moving on to the alto part.

This is how the working will look at this stage:

It now remains to complete the alto part and, as with the tenor, it will be necessary to keep a close eye on the vertical texture and movement of the other lines to see that there is a good overall musical flow.

**Phrase 2**    In bar 3 there are two places which are at present static from one crotchet beat to the next – between beats two and three, and between beat four and the following bar. The latter is easily remedied with a B passing note, but the former requires a little more thought. It would seem obvious to put in a G passing note but you will see that this causes consecutive 5ths with the soprano part. Bach solves the problem by regarding the third-beat chord of A major as a transient modulation to that key and turns his passing note into a G♯, thus producing an acceptable progression of diminished 5th followed by perfect 5th:

**Phrase 3**    You will see that there is already quaver movement in at least one part throughout bar 5:

However, the three crotchet As in the alto part are somewhat dull and repetitive and some improvement in the melodic shape is desirable. An auxiliary note is frequently used to give interest to two repeated notes, but this will not work successfully here. Between the first two As an upward auxiliary will give consecutive 5ths between alto and bass, whilst a lower one will produce consecutive 5ths between alto and soprano. Auxiliary notes between the second and third As will be similarly undesirable, and so Bach takes the bold step of joining the third crotchet A and the following B with a semitone passing note of A♯. This, of course, is the leading note of the key and prepares the cadence which comes in the next bar.

**N.B.**     You will remember that when we were completing the bass line of bar 5 it was decided not to use the perfectly satisfactory musical option of linking the third and fourth beats with two semiquavers (E and F♯). Now that the other parts are complete you will see that to do this would produce the following:

The very dense resultant texture is not completely alien stylistically (though Bach generally avoided such crowding), but the sound at the second quaver of the beat of E–C♯–A♯–E is harsh, and for these two reasons it is preferable to retain a plain crotchet D in the bass.

In bar 6 a passing note B will give a pleasing descending figure in 3rds with the soprano and prevent the rather ugly clash of the soprano D against the alto C♯. The use of simultaneous passing notes producing quaver movement in 3rds or 6ths (or compound intervals of these) is common in Bach's harmonisations and we shall see another example of it in the following bar. His other most common use of simultaneous passing notes is to use them in contrary motion, and an example of this can be seen in the soprano and tenor parts at the beginning of bar 3.

Another characteristic of Bach's style is his frequent unorthodox treatment of the leading note at cadences, and an example of this occurs in bar 6, where the A♯ leading note moves **down** to an F♯. As you will know from harmony books, the leading note is so called because it 'leads' on to the tonic, and leading notes normally move upwards by a semitone. But just as earlier, in bar 4, we saw Bach's concern for melodic shape taking precedence over vertical spacing between the alto and tenor parts, here his wish to have full harmony in final cadence chords frequently takes precedence over his concern for the 'correct' movement of leading notes if the latter results in the 5th of the chord being omitted. He therefore often allows leading notes to fall to the 5th of the final tonic chord or, more rarely, to rise to its 3rd. In this chorale he does this four times – at the end of phrase 1 in the tenor, at the end of bar 4 in the soprano, here at the end of phrase 3 and also in the alto part of the final cadence.

Before moving on to the last phrase one further point needs to be made about bar 6, which is that you should not attempt to put in a passing note between the second and third beats. **This is because Bach's falling leading notes always move directly to the dominant**, and also because of the clash which an intervening passing note would produce with the tenor F♯.

**Phrase 4**     In bar 7 there is clearly a chance to introduce a G♯ passing note between the third and fourth beats:

Between the fourth beat and the first beat of bar 8 we see an apparent false relation – the alto A♮ and the bass A♯. To avoid this the alto must move somewhere on the last quaver of bar 7 – but where? If to another harmony note, it must either move down to an F♯ or a D. The latter would involve crossing below the tenor note, although crossing of inner parts is not infrequent in Bach's harmonisations. What does rule out this option is the unpleasant sound of the alto D against the bass G♯. (The sound of the G♯ against the held D in the soprano is perfectly acceptable; it is the simultaneous arrival on the tritone which is not, and playing the two options should make this immediately apparent to the ear.)

The other choice of harmony note is to jump to an F♯, which could then be tied to the first note of bar 8. The resultant doubling with the tenor F♯ produces a slightly thin sound at the end of the bar but this is acceptable and would probably be the solution adopted by many of us:

Bach's answer is, on the last quaver of bar 7, to use a quaver B. This may be regarded either as a 3rd of a 7th chord on the final quaver beat of the bar, or as a passing note which, on the face of it, does not pass. The effect is to continue the pleasing upward quaver movement in tandem with the bass, and the presence of a C♯ in the soprano part at the beginning of bar 8 tricks the ear into imagining that the alto passing note has moved to this. Indeed, by altering the layout of the parts at the beginning of bar 8 Bach could have doubled the C♯ in the soprano and alto parts. What he chooses to do is to obtain a fuller sound by giving the alto another harmony note (F♯), relying on a kind of aural conjuring trick to cover this unusual melodic procedure. His one other embellishment in bar 8 is to tie the second quaver B to another quaver, thus forming a 4–3 suspension on the first chord of the final cadence:

**A note about suspensions**

Though the suspension in bar 8 is the only example of the device in this particular chorale it is frequently used by Bach to embellish melodic lines, and you should be familiar with its correct use. In essence it consists of delaying the movement of one part when the music moves from one chord to the next. The suspended note forms a dissonance with the other parts as they change to the new chord and then it resolves by step to form a new concord. The two examples below of straight chordal movement (Ex. 1) and chordal movement involving a suspension (Ex. 2) should make this clear:

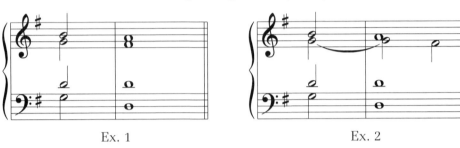

Ex. 1                                        Ex. 2

You will find full explanations of the use of suspensions in any of the standard textbooks on harmony, but for their use in this particular question the following points should be remembered:

1.  The suspended note must be prepared and must resolve **in the same part**.

2.  The actual point of suspension, where the dissonance occurs, must be on a stronger part of the bar than the points of preparation and resolution.

3.  The suspension must resolve **by a step**, either upwards or downwards.

4.  Progressions which are musically unsatisfactory without a suspension are rarely satisfactory with one. This applies particularly to the use of the 9–8 suspension in relation to consecutive octaves, a progression that is best avoided in an exam question:

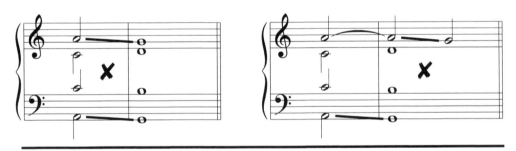

Having completed the alto line, check it for consecutive 5ths and octaves with the three other parts before leaving the question. You will find it quicker and more reliable to do this with each individual line rather than looking vertically at the harmonic movement from beat to beat.

Bach's working, in which you can see that some 'cautionary' accidentals have been added to the bass in bar 3, is printed opposite. In minor-key examples care is always needed with the submediant and leading note notation, depending on whether an ascending or descending form of the melodic minor scale is used.

A chorale in a minor key will (as here) normally end with a tierce de Picardie major chord, but this will always be shown in the harmonic skeleton given on staves **A** and you should not alter, in your working, what is given originally.

▶  **CHECKLIST OF PROCEDURES FOR WORKING A CHORALE-TYPE QUESTION**

- Fix the key of the piece firmly in your mind. If it is minor, be very careful to use correct accidentals for the upward or downward 6ths and 7ths, according to the relevant melodic minor scale.

- Look closely at the given opening, and any fragments of music which may be provided, for any help which they might give in your working.

- Be sure not to alter any of the basic harmony which is set out on staves **A**.

- Do not allow any of your added melodic lines to go above the given soprano or below the given bass parts. Crossing of inner parts is admissible if the result is musically valid.

- Build up your working by completing each vocal line separately, beginning with the soprano (if it is not already given), then the bass, tenor and alto lines, ensuring that they have as much melodic interest as possible.

- As the inner parts are added, keep an eye on the vertical texture of the piece, aiming for flowing but uncongested movement overall, and avoiding too many short-value notes.

- Do not add any embellishments to final notes of the chorale 'phrases', which are indicated by pause chords.

- Do not use any keyboard ornamentation, either as symbols or as written-out notation.

- As you complete each vocal line check it against all other completed parts for consecutives.

- Remember that, at phrase-end cadences, leading notes may fall (usually to the 5th of the following chord) in order to achieve fuller harmony.

- Remember that simultaneous passing notes are quite common in Bach's style. In similar motion they usually move in 3rds or 6ths (including compound 3rds or 6ths): in contrary motion they most frequently occur as a single passing note joining two harmony notes with the passing note being common to both parts, either at the unison, octave or double octave.

- Although (as we have seen) Bach does not always abide by this rule, it is better, in normal practice, not to exceed the interval of an octave between adjacent parts, except between tenor and bass.

- Resist any temptation to make the added parts too ornate.

# Sample Question 2

Let us now consider a contrasting example which is an instrumental extract from the Classical period.

**On the staves marked A below is an outline of a passage from a piano sonata by Haydn, leaving out certain suspensions, passing notes and other notes of melodic decoration. The music on the staves marked B is what the composer actually wrote. Continuing in the same style, reconstruct the blank and partially completed bars.**

## WORKING THE QUESTION

It will be immediately apparent that a question of this type needs a radically different approach from a Bach chorale. The main difference is that with the chorale we were recreating a series of vocal lines, whilst here we are dealing with a keyboard texture which should be dealt with as a whole, bar by bar, though, as you will see, it is sometimes a help to consider the treble and bass staves separately.

We should, however, take the usual first step of being sure in our mind of the key of the extract (A major) and we should note any accidentals which might indicate modulations, such as the main one to E major at bar 8. All modulations and passing changes of key will be indicated by accidentals on staves **A** and we should note that these will have to be incorporated into our working.

Next we should look at the structure of the whole passage. In a Classical extract such as this it is more than likely that the music will conform to a regular phrase structure, and it is advisable to mark in the phrases lightly in pencil. This passage consists of three four-bar phrases.

Having got some idea of the overall structure, look next at the given opening (and take note of any tempo indication) to discover the character of the piece. Here the first four-bar phrase, together with the 'Allegro con brio' marking, gives the impression of lively movement, with a decorative right-hand melody supported by a bass which supplies the underlying harmony mostly in the form of repeated quaver chords. This is the general style and texture which we should try to continue. You will notice a little four-semiquaver fragment which has been inserted at bar 10. This refers to some specific feature at that point of the working. It will be dealt with later in that capacity, but may be noted now as an indication of the general style of the extract.

So far we have a grasp of the key, phrase structure and general character of the passage. The next thing is to look for any specific musical ideas in the given opening which we should make use of later. The repeated-quaver bass figures have already been noted and, if we look at the right-hand part, the little rhythmic figure which appears at the beginning and in bar 2 should strike us as significant. Take note also of its extension in bars 1 to 2, particularly the rhythm:

It is very likely, in the balanced, clear-cut Classical structure with which we are dealing, that this will form the core of the right-hand melody.

**Phrase 2**   With these factors in mind let us now look at the second phrase (bars 4–8). It might be simpler to consider the left-hand part first, as this appears to be more straightforward. Indeed, all that needs to be done is to continue the repeated quaver pattern:

A small but important point which should be noted is that the given opening phrase on staves **B** finishes with a crotchet in bar 4, which means that the repeated quaver figure should not begin until the second half of that bar. In joining your continuation to the end of the given opening you must never interfere with the pitch or rhythm of what is printed on staves **B**. If repeated quavers were intended at the *beginning* of bar 4, the given opening would have implied this by ending as shown left.

Now look at the right-hand part. You will see on stave **A** a two-quaver rising third figure at the beginning which also appears in bar 2. At these places on stave **B** Haydn has written the dotted quaver–two demisemiquaver motif discussed above, and it is logical to expect that the second, answering, phrase will begin in the same way.

A moment ago we noted particularly the rhythm of the extension of the opening motif. Considering our aim to produce a balanced structure it would clearly be desirable to use this rhythmic motif in bar 5, and though the harmonic skeleton here is not the same as in bar 1, the spacing of the notes in bar 5 allows for the gaps to be filled neatly by a descending figure of four semiquavers beginning on E (marked *a* in the music below). This will resemble the earlier group sufficiently closely to be musically satisfactory.

Having pencilled this into your working look next at bars 6 and 7. You will see that their harmonic outline is the same as for bar 5 but at different pitches, and this should suggest to you some form of sequence. So merely by repeating your right-hand melody of bar 5, starting on a B in bar 6 and an A in bar 7, the second phrase is complete, with an effective extension of the opening figure modulating to the dominant key of E major. The first right-hand note of bar 8 could be a straight crotchet E or you could decorate it with a D♯ appoggiatura.

The result will look like this:

Remember to check your working so far for consecutive 5ths and octaves before proceeding to the third phrase:

Look first at the right-hand melody, where the first three notes of the given outline direct you once more to a similar figure to that which was used for the beginning of phrase 2. The two rising quavers certainly call for further use of the dotted quaver–two demisemiquaver motif, but after that you have the choice of either using the repeated quaver figure again or being a little more decorative and introducing a four-semiquaver group at this point, bearing in mind that it would need to be continued to prevent a somewhat bare effect in the second half of the bar. Any of the following would work:

We should take into account, though, the semiquaver group which has been put in at the end of bar 10. This would appear to indicate that the figure should be used again in bar 11, and in view of this it might be better to vary this figure for the preceding bar. What Haydn does is to stick to his opening idea and just decorate the first note of bar 10 with an appoggiatura:

You should not, though, regard this as the only 'correct' answer. For instance, you could have written this, which would have been perfectly satisfactory:

Less satisfactory would have been a phrase like this, in view of the figure which has been cued in at the end of bar 10:

We should now consider the semiquaver group which has been given to us in bar 10 and see how it might affect the remainder of the melodic line. The simplest option would be to use the same figure for the next two crotchets, and the job is done. If it were felt that three successive identical groups were a little monotonous we could invert one of them by jumping up a 3rd to the second semiquaver and then descending to the starting note. This would not be satisfactory at the last beat of bar 11 as consecutive octaves (albeit disguised by an accented passing note) would result. The figure would therefore need to be used at the beginning of bar 11 and the right hand of the two bars would look like this:

What Haydn does, in fact, is to use the same figure three times (as you will see in the completed working overleaf), but again this is not the only acceptable solution; it is merely one of two equally satisfactory options.

The remaining task is to reconstruct the bass line. At present it looks like this, with the completed right-hand part given above it:

All that is needed is to ensure that the left-hand part provides the necessary harmonic support and continues the style established so far, this being principally the use of repeated quaver pairs. Our main decision, then, is whether to use quavers throughout the phrase or whether to give some respite by retaining a single crotchet on occasion. If we choose the latter course the best places for a single crotchet will be where there is semiquaver movement in the right hand and possibly at the mid-point of the phrase, below the upper appoggiatura figure. The first half of the phrase would then appear thus (you will see that it is a form of harmonic suspension: C♯–B and B–A♯):

But bearing in mind the 'Allegro con brio' marking, the piece needs good rhythmic vitality, and the two successive crotchets clearly hold up the repeated quaver figures which are the main means of achieving this. Haydn therefore maintains quaver movement at this point and, indeed, continues it to the end of the phrase.

This is the passage as Haydn wrote it:

▶    **RECOMMENDED STEPS FOR WORKING THIS TYPE OF QUESTION**

- Note the key and any accidentals, together with possible modulations implied by the latter.

- Decide upon the phrase structure and pencil this in lightly.

- Assess the character of the piece from any tempo and performance directions at the beginning, as well as from the appearance of the given opening.

- Work through the passage phrase by phrase from the beginning, looking out for clues to subsequent musical ideas which may be given by the opening supplied on staves **B**, maintaining also the general texture and character of this.

- **Take great care to observe any changes of clef which might occur in the course of the extract.** Failure to do this will obviously lead to severe inaccuracy in your working.

- Look carefully at any fragments of music which may be supplied during the course of the extract. These will principally be giving clues to what might follow but they could also affect your choice of preceding musical figures.

- Do not crowd the texture with too much embellishment.

- In instrumental questions it is possible to use ornamentation signs, **providing that they serve a valid musical purpose**. They should not be used merely to demonstrate to the examiner that you know how to write them, and if you use them at all, do so very sparingly, remembering that one ornament is much more effective than twenty. Above all follow the motto 'if in doubt, leave it out'.

- As you build up your working phrase by phrase, check carefully for consecutives.

The two examples given for this question do not cover all the options which might face you in the exam itself. The syllabus merely refers to 'rewriting a given passage to include appropriate suspensions and notes of melodic decoration'. You could, for instance, be given a passage in short score for string quartet, or some type of three-part instrumental or vocal extract. These would, of course, be linear in character and would need to be worked along the lines suggested for the Bach chorale. But whatever the passage is written for, you can be assured that it will be straightforward and clearly representative of a particular musical style, and a firm grasp of the preceding procedures should enable you to approach it with confidence and efficiency.

(See *Harmony in Practice*, Chapter 14, for comment and exercises on the various additional types of decoration encountered in the Classical period.)

# Question 2   Sample Questions

**The sample questions on pages 38–43 are passages which have been taken or adapted from works by various composers. On the staves marked A is an outline of the extract, leaving out certain suspensions, passing notes and other notes of melodic decoration. The music on the staves marked B is what the composer actually wrote. Continuing in the given style, reconstruct the blank and partially completed bars.**

**1.** J. S. Bach, Chorale: 'Du grosser Schmerzensmann'

**2.** Mozart: Piano sonata in A major, K.331

etc.

**3.** J. S. Bach, Chorale: 'Wenn ich in Angst und Not'

**4.** Haydn: Piano sonata in G major, Hob. XVI/40

**5.** J. S. Bach, Chorale: 'Wo Gott zum Haus nicht gibt'

**6.** Vivaldi: Trio sonata 'La Follia'

(For convenience of working, this extract has been presented in short score.)

**7.** Beethoven: String quartet in A major, Op. 18 No. 5

  (For convenience of working, this extract has been presented in short score.)

**8.** J. S. Bach, Chorale: 'Jesu, du mein liebstes Leben' (adapted)

# Question 3(a)

The syllabus offers a choice between Question 3(a), which is considered here, and Question 3(b), which is covered in the next section of this workbook.

In Question 3(a) of Grade 6 you were asked to continue a melody using a given opening. In Question 3(a) of Grade 7 your ability to write an imaginative, stylish and shapely melody is still being tested, but with the added requirement that it should fit the harmony of a given piano accompaniment.

An extract, or adaptation, of actual music will be used and you will be expected to complete the melody for a named instrument. The extract will always have a clearly defined harmonic structure. You will be given:

1. The start of the melody and possibly other notes or parts later in the extract.

2. The complete piano accompaniment.

3. Some help towards the phrase structure either by means of notes/rests/phrasing written in for you or by guidance in the wording of the question.

4. The name of the instrument for which you should write, the tempo (perhaps even a title) and the name of the composer, with dates where appropriate.

This means that you will already have:

- *The melodic and rhythmic essence of your melody.* This should not be repeated so slavishly that the result is monotonous. However, there may be opportunities for the effective use of exact or near exact repetition when the harmony is repeated. Some effective melodies are static when the accompaniment is active, and vice versa. Simultaneous melodic movement in 3rds and 6ths can be effective between the solo instrument and one part of the accompaniment.

- *The full harmonic basis for your melody.* Look for modulations, cadence points, repetitions of the harmony and sequences. You must take care not to contradict the given harmony in your choice of melody notes, but this does not rule out the effective use of notes of melodic decoration which may cause temporary discord; parallel (consecutive) 5ths and octaves between the melody and bass should be avoided, and any rests in the melody must be observed. These factors will influence the overall shape and balance of the melody.

- *Stimulation to your imagination and encouragement to think in terms of the period and style from which the composer comes.* The practicalities of the named instrument and the effective use of the tempo and any given expressive indications, together with your own playing and preparation of pieces in the given style, should help you to write a shapely and effective melody.

Before considering how to tackle the question it would be of great benefit for you to study carefully a few suitable examples of pieces you have prepared for performance to see the relationship of melody and accompaniment. This does not preclude pianists, who could study suitable songs or simple piano pieces with an independent right-hand melody over an accompaniment. Observe particularly how notes of melodic decoration and ornaments enhance the melodic lines, bringing a sense of style to the music.

Information about notes of melodic decoration, aspects of melody and writing for instruments will be found in Chapters 15, 18 and 19–20 respectively of *The AB Guide to Music Theory*, Part II.

Now we can consider these earlier points and work a sample question, though one which is longer than you would be likely to meet in an exam.

# Sample Question 1

**Complete the violin part of the trio section from Schubert's Sonatina in G minor for violin and piano, D.408. You should construct the melody to form six four-bar phrases.**

**WORKING THE QUESTION**

On looking at the given extract we can see that the opening key is E♭ major and the accompaniment provides a clear harmonic basis consisting mainly of one chord per bar, as follows:

- The harmony alternates between chords I and V$^7$ (or V) in bars 1–6.

- A perfect cadence in the key of B♭ major is implied by the bass at bars 7–8.

- The harmony in bars 9–12 alternates between V (or V$^7$) and i in C minor.

- The harmony in bars 13–16 is a sequence of bars 9–12, now in B♭ major.

- Bars 17–20 repeat bars 1–4, but with V rather than V$^7$ in bar 20.

- The harmony in bars 21–24 has the same pattern as that in bars 5–8, but now in E♭ major.

We can also see that:

- The melody given in bars 1–3 consists of only two rhythms.

- The melody given in bar 16 consists of continuous quavers.

- There are dynamic changes for each eight-bar section.

- The tempo, phrasing, *dolce* and *legato* nature of the violin opening give a clue to the general style.

On a piece of manuscript paper we can sketch in some important possible melody notes which belong to the basic harmony.

(We don't necessarily need to label the chords as we did for Grade 6 because they are given in the accompaniment notes here.)

There is clearly a wide choice of melody notes available from this rhythmically static framework including, on the first beats of bars 7 and 23, the option to use notes from either chord IV, chord ii or chord ii$^7$b. We can now develop our melody by considering the following options:

- Use of different notes of the same chord (as Schubert does in bars 1–3).

- 3rds between the melody and bass in bars 6 and 22 which would strengthen the line. (This can often be helpful when a root position chord is preceded or followed by its first inversion.)

- Repetition of the opening rhythm (bars 1–4) in the second phrase (bars 5–8), to give structural balance.

- Repetition of the melody of bars 1–3 in bars 17–19, as the harmony is the same.

- A melodic sequence to match the harmonic one between bars 9–12 and bars 13–16.

- The use of a transposed version of bars 5–8 in bars 21–24, which would round off the melody most effectively.

These additions are shown below. We now have a balanced phrase structure as stipulated, with clear cadence points and a modulation in bar 8 which we have chosen to approach by a chord of iib rather than IV in bar 7. This gives us some stepwise movement to counteract the jumping in the melody:

There is some rhythmic variety with ♩ ♩, ♩. ♪♩ and ♩ ♩ ♩, as well as ♩. which ends some of the four-bar phrases. The 3rds between the melody and bass in bars 6 and 22 improve on the previous static rhythm of the initial working on pages 46–47. However, it still doesn't look like an expressive melody for violin so we need to add dynamics (from the piano part) and some bowing (based on that used in the given opening):

We now have quite a passable attempt which has balance and shape, but it is interesting to see what Schubert actually wrote (printed opposite). Note:

- how the staccato dots in the accompaniment in bars 7 and 23 have been effectively used in the melody too, and also in bar 11;

- how the use of ornaments brings style and life to the melody;

- how the lower auxiliary notes in bars 11 and 15 and the quaver run in bar 12 give some welcome stepwise motion, particularly with the unaccented passing notes and the attractive chromatic accented passing note (appoggiatura) F♯.

Finally, bear in mind that examiners do not expect you to produce what the composer wrote in order to obtain a very good mark. Your knowledge of playing or singing repertoire from the same period as the piece set will help you greatly with stylistic matters. With this in mind you should have a careful look at the pieces you know, noting the characteristics of that particular style.

A similar way of working is suggested for another short and simple extract, in a different key and metre, by Mozart.

# Sample Question 2

**Complete the violin part in the passage printed overleaf, adapted from the third movement of Mozart's Piano Trio No. 5 in G major, K.564. You should construct the melody to form two four-bar phrases. (In Mozart's original the dynamic is *mf* throughout, and the bowing only slurred at cadences.)**

**WORKING THE QUESTION**

Note:

- the character of the given melodic opening;

- the dotted rhythm and the upper auxiliary note in the given start;

- the neutral, but full, harmonic basis of the accompaniment;

- identical harmony in bars 1–2 and 5–6;

- the chromatic note in bar 3;

- the rests in bar 4 suggesting a cadence;

- the rests in bar 8 suggesting another cadence, this time decorated;

- that you need to complete bar 1.

This example should now be worked following similar procedures to those given for Sample Question 1. The following hints will also help:

- Mozart's melody follows quite closely the outline of the accompaniment top part, which, being off the beat, does not result in direct doubling.

- There is much rhythmic repetition.

- Beware of jumping up and down *too* much between notes of the same chord. (However, some melodies are built on such jumps and you should always look at the given part of the melody for stylistic clues.)

Mozart's own melody is printed on the next page. It shows:

- effective use of the given motif without monotony, including repetition when the harmony repeats, and a mixture of leaps and stepwise motion;

- use of contrary motion between melody and bass;

- clear cadence points, Ic–V (a 'feminine' ending) and V$^7$–I, in a perfectly balanced pair of phrases. (See *Harmony in Practice*, Chapter 7, for more examples of the cadential $^6_4$.)

Finally, here are some of the common faults noted by examiners in the working of this question in general:

- Continuous and consistent doubling (shadowing) of notes in the melodic part of an accompaniment. Sometimes composers do this as part of a longer scheme, particularly an octave higher, but in the extracts set for this question the composer's original will generally avoid this feature.

- Limited range of melodies. Don't be frightened to use the instrument's compass and special effects, provided you are sure that no particular problems are created (see *Theory Workbook Grade 6*, page 30, and *The AB Guide to Music Theory*, Part II, Chapters 19 and 20 for working ranges of the standard instruments).

- Lack of stepwise motion and notes of melodic decoration. Some attempts leap too much while preserving the basic harmony.

- Poor phrase balance.

- Over-use of a given motif, or the reverse which results in meandering lines having no connection with the given start.

- Clashing melody and harmony, often as a result of neglected accidentals.

- Omitted completion of the first bar, or of other bars in which only some of the notes are given.

- A very untidy exam paper, usually because the 'working out' has been done on the staves provided rather than on separate manuscript paper.

The sample questions overleaf will enable you to develop your skills in writing melodies over given accompaniments. They show a variety of keys and metres, and of styles and periods from Baroque to Romantic, and some of the extracts (Sample Questions 5, 6, 7, 8 and 9) lend themselves to more extended practice in one question than would be the case in an exam paper.

# Question 3(a)  Sample Questions

1. Complete the violin part in this extract adapted from the third movement of Mozart's Piano Trio No. 5 in G major, K.564. You should construct the melody to form four two-bar phrases. (Note the keys – this extract is from later in the same movement as the Mozart worked in this chapter.)

2. Complete the violin part in this extract from Beethoven's Sonata Op. 12 No. 1. You should construct the melody to form two four-bar phrases.

3. Complete the oboe part in this arrangement of Schubert's song *Adieu*. You should construct the melody to form four two-bar phrases.

4. Complete the clarinet part in this extract which is taken from the Duo Op. 15 by N. Burgmüller (1810–1836), a contemporary of Schumann. The rests on the clarinet stave indicate the phrase structure you should use, but remember to fill in the incomplete bars. The clarinet part is printed at concert pitch.

5.  Complete the trumpet part in this arrangement of Schubert's song *The Shepherd's Lament*. Marks
    have been inserted above the trumpet stave to indicate the phrase structure which you should use.
    The trumpet part is printed at concert pitch.

etc.

**6.** Complete the violin part in this extract from Beethoven's Sonata Op. 12 No. 3. You should construct the melody to form two four-bar phrases in each of the two sections.

7. Complete the clarinet part in these extracts from the Concerto Op. 26 No. 1 by Spohr (1784–1859). Marks have been inserted above the clarinet stave to indicate the phrase structure which you should use. The clarinet part is printed at concert pitch; the piano part is a reduction of the original orchestral accompaniment.

8.  Complete the flute part in this extract taken from the Gavotte from *Sonata for flute and basso continuo* Op. 2 No. 5 by the French composer Michel Blavet (1700–1768). You should construct the melody to form three four-bar phrases, two two-bar phrases and a four-bar phrase.

9. Complete the horn part in this extract which has been adapted from a song by Carl Loewe (1796–1869). The given notes and rests show the phrase lengths. The horn part is printed at concert pitch.

etc.

# Question 3(b)

In this alternative to Question 3(a) *either* you are asked to write a melody based on a given progression of chords *or* you are asked to continue a given melodic figure, depending on the exam paper.

## Using a given chord progression

For this type of question:

- You will usually be asked to write an eight-bar melody.

- Either one instrument will be specified, or you will be given a choice between two specified instruments.

- Each given chord will contain three or four notes, and the given material will be written in either the treble or bass clef (unless any of the given material is for viola, in which case an alto C clef will be used).

- You will be required to use either one or two chords per bar.

- The chords will be limited to those in the syllabus.

- Modulation and/or sequences will often be included.

- A clear harmonic framework will be evident.

- You will also be given a melodic opening which you can, if you wish, use to start your melody.

## Sample Question

This is taken from the *Specimen papers*, but there you are asked to write for unaccompanied oboe.

**Compose a lively melody of eight bars in length for unaccompanied flute. Form your melody from the chord progression below, using one chord for each bar, together with any diatonic or chromatic decorations you consider appropriate. You may use the given opening or not, as you prefer. Write your complete melody on the staves below.**

**WORKING THE QUESTION**

We can see that the chord framework:

- is in B♭ major;

- has chord vi at bar 4 which could make a good cadence point;

- has a dominant 7th – tonic ending;

- does not imply modulation.

As the chords, and therefore the harmonic structure, are so clearly set out, labelling may not be necessary. But you will notice that some of the chords have four notes and, if it helps you to think harmonically, there is no reason why you should not label these:

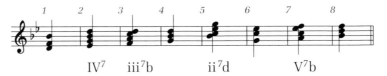

The aim is to compose a shapely line which is idiomatic to the flute and has a well-balanced phrase structure, rhythmic, expressive and dynamic interest, and a lively character. You don't *have* to use all the notes in each chord in each bar and they do not need to be in any particular order.

A basic attempt, of the type sometimes marked by examiners, can be seen in **Version A**. The fundamental harmony is correct, the phrase structure is balanced and the melody is suitable for the flute, even though it does not look particularly instrumental.

**Version A**

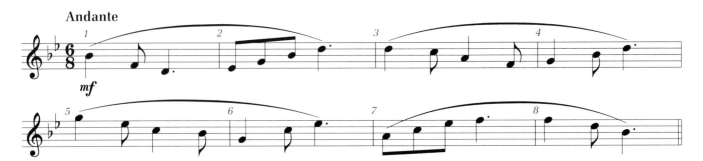

However, it has several faults:

- It is rhythmically unimaginative, using only ♩ ♪, ♩. and ♫♩ patterns.

- It does not develop any rhythmic or melodic motif to give it unity.

- The given notes are used too literally, going up or down the notes of the chords in order.

- No notes other than those of the chords are used.

- It is placid, rather than lively.

- There are no rests, though the phrase marks would allow breathing spaces.

- There are no appropriate expression marks and only the one given dynamic.

- The repeated F in the last bar would have to be tongued again, but it is slurred here.

In spite of these faults it still has some good melodic qualities in the rise and fall of the line and in its 'singability'. Sing it through if possible, choosing a suitable pitch. If not, play it. If a gentle, 'pastorale' style melody had been wanted, this could have been a useful start.

**Version B** below shows more rhythmic imagination and life. We have used the given opening here, which has slurred notes, repeated notes and a dotted rhythm. Bars 3 and 7 use the rhythm and articulation of bar 1, and bar 5 is rhythmically identical to bar 2. The use of these rhythmic motifs helps unify the melody. The ascending and descending motion of the line in bars 5–8 is a big improvement, even though no notes of melodic decoration are used. We now have breathing spaces, though the higher range of the flute has not been used and we could make the melody still more lively.

**Version B**

In all your melodic writing you should try to 'hear' the intervals whenever this is practical and you should always imagine the line being played on the named instrument. Playing the melodies through after you've written them is very helpful and instructive, particularly when learning how to answer this type of question.

Notice how **Version C** below builds on **Version B** in the following ways:

**Version C**

- The first added notes in bar 2 create a new and quite lively rhythm as well as some stepwise movement through the use of unaccented passing notes.

- The dotted rhythm is used in bars 4 and 5, and also in bar 8 where it contains an arpeggio on the tonic chord in the top register of the flute.

- Bars 5 and 6 now contain more semiquaver movement and a wider pitch range, including arpeggiated notes of the chord and the use of the added rhythm and stepwise movement introduced in bar 2.

- The melody still adheres closely to the given chords, but the harmony notes – used on the strong beats of the bar – are interspersed with notes of melodic decoration.

- The articulation is varied, and uses the slurred and staccato patterns given, which are very effective on the flute.

- The dynamics are also varied, according to the intended effects in the different registers.

- The gentle liveliness of the given opening is retained in a melody which is suitable for, and effective on, the flute.

Play this melody through and you will notice that there is plenty of interest in its shape, dynamics, articulation and phrasing.

In **Version D** below we can see a still more lively approach but this time, to give an example of writing for a different instrument, we have imagined that the question asks us to write for the clarinet. This version does not use the given start, and you will notice that:

- It has a faster tempo.

- It still adheres closely to the given harmonic framework.

- It exploits the lower pitch range effectively.

- It contains a lot of staccato and a little slurred articulation.

- Bars 3 and 7 begin with rests which help to create an element of surprise and a playful and lively character, particularly when alongside sudden dynamic changes and staccato tonguing.

- There is less stepwise movement than in **Version C** for flute.

- There is plenty of dynamic interest and an effective use of register contrasts.

- Bars 5 and 6 invert the shape of bars 1 and 2, using the same rhythm, and this helps to unify the melody.

- The grace notes bring a humorous touch to the style, and, though some of them are chromatic, their use does not obscure the harmonic basis.

**Version D**

Play it through, then play **Version C** again.

Comparing **Versions C** and **D** shows two interesting general points:

1. A given start carries some limitations, in that it introduces a style and motifs that need to be developed if the melody is to be convincing. However, it is a safe basis, particularly for those who are less experienced.

2. 'Starting from scratch' as in **Version D** can be particularly rewarding for those with more experience of melodic writing and a more detailed knowledge of instrumental matters.

Faults commonly encountered by examiners in this question and melodic writing in general are:

- Meandering lines that have little or no connection with the chords or the given opening.

- Melodies which are rhythmically limited and too arpeggiated melodically, based on the chord notes only.

- Absence of expression, dynamic and articulation marks.

- Lack of practicality for the instrument, sometimes using notes outside its range.

- Lack of a clear phrase structure.

- Bars containing too many or too few beats (frequently seen).

- Overuse of a given motif, sometimes repeating it every bar.

- Overuse of technical instructions, e.g. pizz./arco changes which are often impractical (giving no time for change).

- No opportunities for breathing in melodies for wind instruments.

- Continuation of the opening rather than the *complete* melody being written on the staves.

- Forgetting to name the chosen instrument when a choice is given.

- Untidy exam paper, through not using manuscript paper for preparatory work.

The examiners will not be expecting advanced compositional skills but they will expect an ability to work a motif (either the given one or one of your own invention) with some musicality on the harmonic framework given, and to show some imagination and practicality in a well structured line.

A study of the melodies which you enjoy playing on your own instrument could help in the development of your skill in writing for other instruments. In this connection Chapters 19–20 of *The AB Guide to Music Theory*, Part II, will give much helpful advice. Chapters 15 and 18, on notes of melodic decoration and aspects of melody respectively, also contain much useful and relevant information for this question. There is no better way of learning than to hear your melodies played, so be prepared to contact your friends, and be willing to play their melodies too.

# Sample Questions

**Compose suitable melodies of eight bars in length for the unaccompanied instruments named. Form your melodies from the chord progressions given, using the chords for each bar, together with any diatonic or chromatic decorations you consider appropriate. You may use the given openings or not, as you prefer. Write the complete melodies on the staves below.**

For further practice, vary the instruments and clefs used. You will often arrive at very different results.

1.   Fanfare for trumpet (concert pitch)                    **Marziale**

2.   Elegy for horn (concert pitch)                         **Adagio**

*or*   Elegy for viola                                      **Adagio**

3.   Sarabande for violin or oboe     Instrument ...................

4.   Country Dance for clarinet (concert pitch)

5.   Solemn March for trombone

**6.**    Pastorale for flute

**7.**    Burlesque for bassoon

**8.**    Waltz for cello

# Continuing a given melodic figure

In many ways this is similar to:

- using the given opening and basing the melody on a progression of chords, the difference here being that you are not restricted by a given harmonic structure;

- the modern style melodic composition option (Question 3(b)) in Grade 6.

Consequently much of the advice given under these two previous headings is relevant here and we should consider this when working the following question which was set in Paper 1999A.

# Sample Question

**Compose a complete piece of not less than eight bars for unaccompanied horn (at concert pitch) or trombone, based on the given opening. Include appropriate performance directions for the instrument of your choice and state below which it is.**

We will work this opening for trombone and consider the horn later.

**WORKING THE QUESTION**

A careful study of the given melodic figure is important, and we can see that:

- it is based on one rhythm;

- it is clearly in C major in spite of the chromatic appoggiatura in bar 1;

- it consists of leaps around notes of the tonic chord;

- bar 2 is an inverted melodic shape of bar 1;

- the articulation features accented repeated notes and a slurred pattern;

- it is lively and vigorous, with a loud dynamic.

We must imagine how a trombone would sound and pitch the notes in our heads as far as possible when composing our melody. Quite clearly the rhythmic drive of the opening needs to be maintained, though we must take care to avoid monotony through over-repetition. The inclusion of a syncopated rhythm such as ♪ ♩ ♪ would help to do this and create some variety while still maintaining the style and rhythmic drive.

    The question asks for a piece of 'not less than eight bars', and an eight-bar melody is usually the most straightforward to write. However, we will consider a 12-bar melody here. We will introduce sequence and modulation and, importantly, we will build our melody on a firm harmonic foundation.

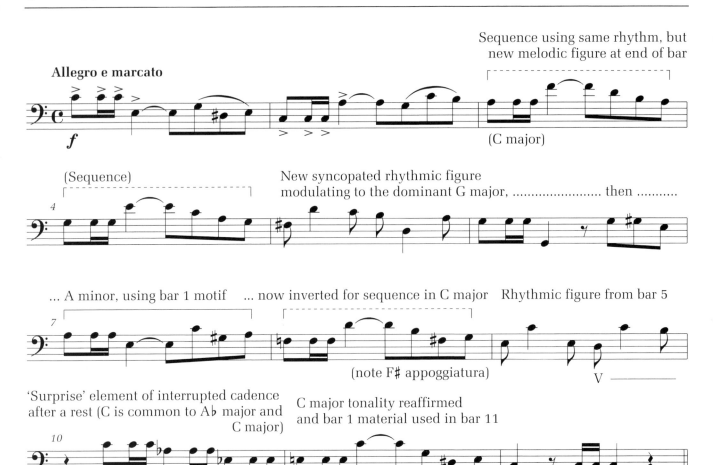

We now have quite a strong, rhythmic melody with a firm harmonic basis, including some variety of key. The phrases are balanced and the line has some melodic interest for the player.

The complete version is set out below with varied dynamics, articulation and phrasing added. We could have used a mute, for some tonal variety, but rests would have been needed to accommodate this, and the relentless rhythmic nature of the short, strong melody might have been disrupted by the inclusion of too many rests (though bar 6 has been adapted to provide a longer rest, for breathing).

If you are short of time you may prefer to write an eight-bar melody. You may decide that a shorter melody is more appropriate anyway, and we shall work on one now. Much of the material we have worked for trombone is also suitable for horn. However, remember that we need to write at concert pitch and that the horn can play higher than the trombone: its usual top sounding note is ♩ but avoid overworking the top register.

Here is a possible eight-bar melody for horn:

**Allegro e marcato**

In the following sample questions you can write for all the named instruments, and for still further practice you can work any of the openings for any suitable instrument. The results can often be surprisingly different according to the different capabilities of the instruments, though you should always maintain the style of the given opening.

It is a good idea to play your workings when you have finished them and, better still, ask any friends who play the actual instruments to play them for you. You will quickly appreciate the importance of writing melodies which are idiomatic to the particular instrument and you will develop your ear and imagination as well. Remember that the common faults encountered by examiners (see page 63) are equally relevant here. Finally, get used to doing your preparatory sketches on manuscript paper, which is provided in the exam. Some candidates try out their ideas on the blank staves which are actually intended for the *final* version. A neat, clear attempt will always make a good initial impression.

# Sample Questions

Compose complete pieces of not less than eight bars for the unaccompanied instruments named, based on the given openings. Include appropriate performance directions for the instruments stated in your choice.

1.    Flute or oboe

     Instrument ..........................

2.    Trumpet or horn (concert pitch)

     *or* viola

     Instrument ..........................

3.    Cello or bassoon

      Instrument ...........................

**Andante espressivo**

4.    Trombone, tuba or double bass

      Instrument ...........................

**Allegro giocoso**

5.    Violin or clarinet (concert pitch)

      Instrument ...........................

**Allegro scherzando**

**6.**    Clarinet or trumpet (concert pitch)

Instrument ...........................

**7.**    Cello or bassoon

Instrument ...........................

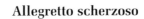

**8.**    Violin, flute or oboe

Instrument ...........................

# Question 4

As in Grade 6, you will be given a passage of music and will be asked a number of questions which test both your understanding of it and your ability to apply the theoretical knowledge you have acquired. While the syllabus for the question remains the same as for Grade 6, the greater range of harmonic vocabulary at Grade 7 (see page 2) opens up the scope of questions under this heading.

At the same time, more emphasis may be placed on your ability to reason, using your greater theoretical knowledge, while still showing your understanding by answering the usual factual questions on the 'nuts and bolts' evident in the extracts. You should also expect more questions on stylistic aspects, performance instructions, and technical features such as structure and the terms associated with it – canon, hemiola, etc.

The information under the various headings listed in the preface to Question 4 of *Theory Workbook Grade 6* should be read again, since this is equally relevant to Grade 7.

A wide range of extracts is possible, occasionally using up to four staves, though the most frequently set medium in recent papers has been the two-stave system for keyboard. Transposing instruments and instruments that use a C clef may also be encountered here.

## Question 4   Sample Questions

Here are a number of tests such as you would find in an exam. As in the Grade 6 workbook, more questions are asked about each extract than would be in an exam, apart from the first extract, which shows how sample marks add up to the usual total of 25. **Occasionally, one slightly longer extract with questions worth a total of 50 marks may be used to cover the ground included in Questions 4 and 5.**

A variety of styles, nationalities and periods is included, and the presentation and wording of the questions is representative of what has been asked in recently set papers.

As before, some of the extracts will be familiar. This does not make them any less relevant, but merely shows how readily available material, including pieces set for the ABRSM practical exams, can be a useful ground for study.

In the same way as comparative performances in the practical exams will require greater technique and interpretative understanding, so will Grade 7 advance beyond Grade 6 in the theory of music.

1. Study the piano piece printed opposite, the second movement of a sonata (*c*.1779) [25] by Samuel Arnold, and then answer the questions below.

(a) Mark clearly on the score, using the appropriate capital letter for identification, one example of each of the following **in the second section**. Also give the bar numbers of your answers.

   A  a 7–6 suspension in the left hand.   Bar(s) ...32..... (3)

   B  a Neapolitan 6th chord.   Bar(s) ...29..... (3)

   C  a $^6_4$–$^5_3$ (Ic–V) progression at an imperfect cadence in C major.   Bar(s) 25....26 (3)
      *G C E     G B D*

(b) Write out in full, as you think it should be played, the top line of the right-hand part of bars 15 and 27.

bar 15

bar 27

(4)

(c) Draw a circle around each of the right-hand non-harmony notes in bars 30–31. (3)

(d) Study the relationship between bars 1–16 and 17–32 and point out **two** similarities and **two** differences between them.

   Similarities  1.  ...similar  rhythms - e.g.  1 & 17  have same rhythm...

             2.  .....................................................................................

   Differences  1.  .....................................................................................

             2.  ..................................................................................... (4)

(e) Complete the following statements:

   The phrase structure is regular, with the length of each phrase being .......... or .......... bars.

   The first imperfect cadence in the piece is to be found in bar .........., and the perfect cadence

   at bars 15–16 is decorated with a ...................................................... . From C major at the start

   of bar 33, the tonality moves first towards the key of .................................... and then towards

   its related key of .................................... in bar 35. (5)

**2.** Study the song printed opposite and then answer the questions below.

A translation of the words:

*Is it true? Is it true that you are always there in the foliage on the vine terrace, waiting for me? And that you are asking the moonlight and the tiny stars about me? Is it true? Tell me! The way I feel can only be understood by she who shares that feeling and who remains true to me forever.*

**(a)** Identify the chords marked * in bars 3, 18, 19 and 20 by writing on the dotted lines below. Use either words or symbols. State the position of each chord, whether it is major, minor, augmented or diminished, and give the prevailing key of each.

bar 3 .................................................     bar 18 .................................................

bar 19 ................................................     bar 20 .................................................

**(b)** Mark clearly on the score, using the appropriate capital letter for identification, one example of each of the following **in bars 1–13**. Also give the bar numbers of your answers.

**A**    a double appoggiatura in the piano part.    Bar ............

**B**    a falling chromatic semitone in the vocal line.    Bar(s) ............

**in bars 14–24**

**C**    a $^6_4$–$^5_3$ (IVc–I) progression on the **tonic** in the piano part.    Bar(s) ............

**D**    a one-bar sequence a 3rd higher than the bar before in the vocal line.    Bar ............

**(c)** Describe the use of the opening motif during the rest of the song. Give bar numbers.

...................................................................................................................................

...................................................................................................................................

...................................................................................................................................

...................................................................................................................................

...................................................................................................................................

...................................................................................................................................

**(d)** Complete the following statements:

The song is in the key of ........................... . When it appears that the music is about to modulate to

the key of ........................ in bars 11–12, a ..................... chord moves to the key of .......................

in bar 12. There is a modulation in bars 16–17 to the key of ........................ and the music passes

through the key of ........................ in bars 17–18.

**(e)** Who of the following do you think is the composer of this song?

Haydn       Alban Berg       Mendelssohn       J. S. Bach       ............................

Give the reasons for your choice.

...................................................................................................................................

...................................................................................................................................

**3.**    Study the extract printed opposite and then answer the questions below.

**(a)**  Show the phrase structure by drawing ⌐⎯⎯⎯⎯⎯⎤ over each of the phrases.

**(b)**  Identify the chords marked * in bars 2, 6, 10, 12 and 21 by writing on the dotted lines below. Use either words or symbols. State the position of each chord, whether it is major, minor, augmented or diminished, and give the prevailing key of each.

bar 2   .................................................          bar 6   .................................................

bar 10  .................................................          bar 12  .................................................

bar 21  .................................................

**(c)**  Write out in full the top line of the right-hand part in bars 3 and 15 as you think it should be played.

bar 3                                                          bar 15

**(d)**  Mark clearly on the score, using the appropriate capital letter for identification, one example of each of the following. Also give the bar numbers of your answers.

**A**    an upward, chromatic appoggiatura in the right-hand part.   Bar ............

**B**    a chromatic lower auxiliary note in the right-hand part in the second section.   Bar ............

**C**    a supertonic chord in first inversion in the first section.   Bar(s) ............

**D**    a $_4^6$–$_3^5$ (Ic–V) progression on the **dominant** at an imperfect cadence between bars 16 and 24.
         Bar(s) ............

**E**    the harmonic interval of a compound major 6th between the top and bottom parts in the
         first section.   Bar(s) ............

**F**    the harmonic interval of an augmented 5th between two left-hand notes in the second
         section.   Bar(s) ............

**(e)**  Trace the keys after the double-bar by completing the following statements:
         The first chord in bar 10 is the first inversion of the dominant chord in the key of ..........................,
         and in bar 11 the music modulates to .............................. . In bars 12–13 the music passes through
         the key of ................................. before coming to a(n) ................................. cadence in the key of
         ............................... in bar 15.

**(f)**  Name **two** differences between bars 1–9 and 16–24.

1.   ...................................................................................................................................

2.   ...................................................................................................................................

**(g)**  From this list of composers, underline the one you think may have written this piece.

                    Haydn        Handel        Schubert        Chopin

Give the reasons for your choice.   ...................................................................................
...................................................................................................................................

4.   Study the first movement of Galuppi's Sonata in D Op. 1 No. 4 (1750), printed opposite, and then answer the questions below.

(a)  Identify the chords marked * in bars 3, 5 and 14 by writing on the dotted lines below. Use either words or symbols. State the position of each chord, whether it is major, minor, augmented or diminished, and give the prevailing key of each.

bar 3   ..............................................................          bar 5   ..............................................................

bar 14   ..............................................................

(b)  Mark clearly on the score, using the appropriate capital letter for identification, one example of each of the following **in the right-hand part**. Also give the bar numbers of your answers.

A    a passage of half a bar repeated sequentially twice, a note lower each time

(draw [         A         ] over the whole passage).   Bars ............

B    a note of anticipation in the first section.   Bar ............

C    an appoggiatura in the first section.   Bar ............

D    a changing note in the first section.   Bar ............

E    a melodic interval of a diminished 3rd, falling, in the second section.   Bar(s) ............

F    a melodic interval of a minor 7th, falling, in the second section.   Bar(s) ............

**and in the left-hand part**:

G    a chromatic lower auxiliary note in the first section.   Bar ............

H    a 7–6 suspension in the second section (draw [ H ] over the notes).   Bar(s) ............

(c)  Draw a circle around each of the non-harmony notes in the right-hand part of bar 5.

(d)  Name the intervals between the lowest and highest notes in the right-hand part of:

bar 11   ..............................................................          bar 14   ..............................................................

(e)  Draw [                    ] over each of the right-hand phrases in the first section to show the phrase structure.

(f)  Complete the following sentences:

The piece begins in D major but modulates to the key of ..................................... in bars 4–5 with

a(n) ............................. cadence in bar 6. In the left-hand part of bar 6, a ............................. on the

dominant of this new key is introduced and the left hand also has examples of .............................

between this point and the middle of bar 8.

(g)  Write out in full the right-hand parts in the following locations as you think they should be played:

bar 1, beats 1–2                    bar 11, beat 3                    bar 15, beat 2

(h)  Compare the two sections of the piece by naming **one** similarity and **one** difference.

Similarity    ..............................................................................................................................

Difference    ..............................................................................................................................

5.  Study the extract from the *Ballade* (No. 1 from *Four Characteristic Pieces*) by William Hurlstone (1876–1906), printed opposite, and then answer the questions below.

(a) Mark clearly on the score, using the appropriate capital letter for identification, one example of each of the following. Also give the bar numbers of your answers.

**A**   a 7th chord on the sharpened submediant of G minor.   Bar(s) ...........

**B**   a Neapolitan 6th chord over a tonic pedal in the piano part.   Bar(s) ...........

**C**   a modulation to B♭ major.   Bar(s) ...........

(b) **(i)**   Point out three appearances of the opening motif during the rest of the extract, giving bar numbers and the instrument concerned.

    1.   .........................................................................................................................................

    2.   .........................................................................................................................................

    3.   .........................................................................................................................................

   **(ii)**  How are bars 9–10 and 11–12 related to this theme?   .................................................

   **(iii)** Which two bars of the last eight bars of the piano part are also related to the theme?

        Bars .................

(c) Write out the part for the clarinet in bars 17–19 as it would sound at concert pitch. Use the appropriate clef and key signature.

(d) Identify the chords marked * in bars 1, 3, 4, 7, 12 and 14 by writing on the dotted lines below. Use either words or symbols. State the position of each chord and whether it is major, minor, augmented or diminished. Treat all the chords as in G minor.

    bar 1   .............................................    bar 3   .............................................

    bar 4   .............................................    bar 7   .............................................

    bar 12  .............................................    bar 14  .............................................

(e) Name **three** ways in which the composer develops intensity in the climactic bars 13–17.

    1.   .........................................................................................................................................

    2.   .........................................................................................................................................

    3.   .........................................................................................................................................

(f) Answer **TRUE** or **UNTRUE** to each of the following statements:

   **(i)**   There are no syncopated entries in the clarinet part.   .............................

   **(ii)**  The lowest note sounded at concert pitch by the clarinet in bar 17 is in unison with the very last right-hand note of the piano in bar 17.   .............................

   **(iii)** There is a plagal cadence in the relative major in bars 7–8.   .............................

6.　Study the extracts printed on pages 84–86 from the *Little Variations on a Russian Theme* Op. 8 No. 14 by Maykapar (1867–1938), and then answer the questions below each extract.

**(a)** What is unusual about the phrase lengths of this theme? .................................................................

**(b)** Describe how the theme, or part of it, is varied in bars 15–30 by completing the statements:

The theme appears ***pp*** in the ................... part with the rising 6th now appearing as a ...........................

in bar 17. From bar 15 the texture is in ........................... and the speed is ..................................... .

Bars 23–26 show ........................... rhythm in the right-hand chords. In bars 27–30 the ...................

phrase of the theme returns to the ................... part but a(n) ................ lower than the theme in pitch.

**(c)** Identify a harmonised imperfect cadence in the section above by drawing ⌐‾‾‾‾‾¬ under the bars.

**(d)** Describe how the theme, or part of it, is varied in this section by completing the statements:

In bars 40–54 there is a strict ..................... between the hands at the distance of a ............... and

the interval of a(n) .................. . The speed is now the same as the ......................... . In bars 55–60

the opening figure of the theme is used but is now in the ................... key, ................... in pace and

..................... in touch with the special effect of the ......................... varying the tone and dynamics.

**(e)** Name three ways by which the second half of the theme is treated/varied in bars 68–79.

1.  ........................................................................................................................................

........................................................................................................................................

2.  ........................................................................................................................................

........................................................................................................................................

3.  ........................................................................................................................................

........................................................................................................................................

**(f)** Which two bars include the top three notes of the melodic minor scale, ascending and descending?

Bars ............... .

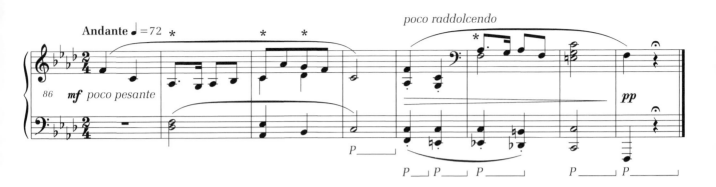

**(g)** Describe how the theme, or part of it, is varied in bars 86–93 by completing the statements:

The tempo here means ........................................................ , the key is ........................ , the touch

quite ........................ and legato at first, then ....................-legato. This is a harmonised version of

the ................... half of the theme but ending with a(n) .................................... cadence and with

the dynamics .................................... .

**(h)** Mark clearly on the score, using the appropriate capital letter for identification, one example of each
of the following in bars 86–93. Also give the bar numbers of your answers.

**A**    a lower auxiliary note.    Bar ............

**B**    the harmonic interval of an augmented 6th between two left-hand notes.    Bar(s) ............

**(i)** Identify the chords marked * in bars 87, 88 and 91 by writing on the dotted lines below. Use either
words or symbols. State the position of each chord and whether it is major, minor, augmented or
diminished. Treat them all as in the key of F minor.

bar 87        ................................................................

bar 88 (first quaver)    ...........................................

bar 88 (third quaver)    ...........................................

bar 91        ................................................................

# Question 5

The syllabus statement remains the same for this question as it was for Grade 6. It would therefore be useful to read page 58 of the Grade 6 workbook, bearing in mind the greater harmonic vocabulary required at Grade 7 and the information given below.

For Grade 6 there were some limitations concerning both the normal size of score and the transposing instruments likely to be included. Now the instrumental and/or vocal resources used could expand beyond the earlier normal maximum of nine staves in a system, and the range of transpositions (e.g. for horns and trumpets) can be expected to enlarge too. However, there is no stipulation that large forces must be used and the questions can be appropriately searching for Grade 7 when smaller forces are used. The information on instrumental matters in *The AB Guide to Music Theory*, Part II Chapters 19–22 will be helpful.

Most questions will include some transposition and will test your knowledge of the 'nuts and bolts' of orchestral scores. As in Question 4, more ability to reason and show knowledge of stylistic aspects will be expected at this grade.

Questions 4 and 5 in any one exam paper will normally complement each other, so, while questions on chord identification and marking phrase structure are less *likely* here than in Question 4, they remain valid areas for testing when appropriate.

## Question 5  Sample Questions

The extract for this question could come from a broad range of periods and styles, from Baroque to the present day, as shown in the sample questions which follow, which are representative of the kind of wording used and the typical requirements of recently set papers. The first sample question shows how the marks might be allocated to arrive at the normal total of 25, but the others often contain many more questions than might be encountered in an exam in order to gain maximum benefit from the printed extracts.

As for Grade 6, intensive study of short, suitable extracts with the score, followed by repeated study of recorded performances, will be an ideal preparation.

1. Study the extract (printed on pages 89–90) from the orchestral opening of the *Burleske* for piano and orchestra by Richard Strauss, then answer the questions below. 25

(a) Give the meaning of:

Kleine Flöte     ................................................     (1)

4 Pauken     ................................................     (1)

Bratsche     ................................................     (1)

(b) (i) Write out the parts for clarinets, bassoons and horns in bars 18–19 as they would sound at concert pitch. Use the staves, clefs and key signature given at the foot of page 90.     (8)

(ii) State two other instruments used in these two bars which do not sound at the written pitch, giving the sounding interval from the written note.

   1.   Instrument ............................. sounding ........................................ than written.

   2.   Instrument ............................. sounding ........................................ than written.     (4)

(c) Mark clearly on the score, using the appropriate capital letter for identification, one example of each of the following. Also give the bar numbers of your answers.

A   a chromatic lower auxiliary note in a string part.   Bar ............     (2)

B   syncopation in a brass part (mark ⌐       **B**       ⌐).   Bar(s) ............     (2)

C   a plucked major 3rd followed by a bowed major 6th in the same instrumental part.

   Bar(s) ............     (2)

(d) Complete the following statements:     (4)

(i) The opening theme is unusual in that it is played by ............................. ;

   it appears again in bars .................... .

(ii) The part for double basses in bars 5–6 sounds as if it could be written in ........... time.

(iii) The melodic fragment played by *pauken* in bar 17 also appears in a different part in

   bar ....... .

**2.** Study the extract printed below from Saint-Saëns' *Danse Macabre,* and then answer the questions on pages 92–93.

[Mouvement modéré de Valse]

**(a)** Give the meaning of:

Grosse caisse   ......................................................................

Timbales   .........................................................................

**Mouvement modéré de Valse**   ..................................................................................................

1°   (oboe, bar 3)   .........................................................

⌢  *très long, toujours en dim.* (bar 17)   .........................................................................

+   (horn III, bar 22)   ......................................................

**(b)** Using the appropriate key signature, write out the parts as they would sound at concert pitch for:

clarinets, bars 39–40

I. II

horns, bars 21–27

III. IV

**(c)** **(i)** Write out the part in full for the solo violin in bars 29–30:

    **(ii)** How many bow-strokes would the player use to perform these bars as marked?   ..........

**(d)** Mark clearly on the score, using the appropriate capital letter for identification, one example of each of the following. Also give the bar numbers of your answers.

    **A**    the harmonic interval of a minor 10th between two of the same instruments.   Bar(s) ...........

    **B**    a note which can only be played on an open string.   Bar(s) ...........

    **C**    a double-stopped perfect 4th.   Bar(s) ...........

    **D**    the start of a four-bar melodic sequence, a 3rd lower than on its first appearance.   Bar .........

**(e)** Describe how the composer releases the tension in bars 8–18 by completing the following statements:

In the dynamics for strings there is a gradual ..................................... from .............. to .............. .

The percussion, busy at first, is reduced in bar ....... and only plays one ...................... per bar from

bar 14, the rhythm becoming more ................... . The chromatic chord throughout on the strings

resolves to a ............... chord on the ............................... note, releasing the harmonic tension, as

does the change in note-lengths from ........................................... to a crotchet in bar 18.

**(f)** Describe what happens melodically and rhythmically in the string parts of bars 32–38 by completing the following statements:

First, the cellos and violas in octaves play a short melody in quaver rhythm. The last ....... notes of

this melody are repeated a(n) .................. higher than the violas by the ........................................ ,

using the same rhythm. In bar 35 the .......................................... then take over these same notes,

a(n) ............... higher still, but in ....................... rhythm, giving the effect of ............................. .

Finally, this group of notes is ............................ by pizzicato basses.

**(g)** Which instruments from the standard 19th-century orchestra do not appear in the extract?

    Brass     ....................................................................................................................................

    Percussion   .............................................................................................................................

3.  Study the extract from Rossini's 'William Tell' Overture, printed opposite, and then answer the questions below.

(a)  Give the meaning of:

**Andantino** ...................................................................................................................................

div. pizz. (viola, bar 1) ...................................................................................................................

a 2 (horns, bar 17) .........................................................................................................................

(b)  Using the appropriate key signature, write out the parts as they would sound at concert pitch for:

(i)  the cor anglais and the horn in E in bars 11–15

(ii)  the clarinets and bassoons in bars 16–20, using the bass clef for bassoons

clarinets

bassoons

(c)  Looking at the parts for strings, identify the chords in bars 11, 12 and 13 by writing on the dotted lines below. Use either words or symbols. State the position of each chord and whether it is major, minor, augmented or diminished.

State the key of the passage .......................................

bar 11 ...............................................    bar 12 ...............................................

bar 13 (first beat) .............................    bar 13 (third beat) ...........................

(d)  Mark clearly on the score, using the appropriate capital letter for identification, one example of each of the following. Also give the bar numbers of your answers.

A  grace notes.  Bar(s)  ............

B  a falling interval of a diminished 5th in a woodwind part between bars 11 and 20.

Bar(s)  ............

C  a bar in which one string instrument plucks a double-stop of a minor 6th interval, then a major 6th.  Bar  ............

D  a changing note in the flute part.  Bar  ............

(e)  (i)  Which standard orchestral woodwind instrument does not play here?  ...............................

(ii)  How does that instrument produce its sound?  .......................................................................

(iii) Which clef does it use?  .................................

(f)  The extract has a peaceful, pastoral quality. How does the composer achieve this?

..........................................................................................................................................................

..........................................................................................................................................................

4.  Study the extract from the later stages of R. Vaughan Williams' *Serenade to Music* for voices and orchestra, printed opposite, and then answer the questions below.

(a) Give the meaning of:

**sostenuto**  ..............................................................................................................................

*sempre con sord.*  .......................................................................................................................

naturale (previously 'harm.') (harp, bar 10)  ............................................................................

unis. (violin 2, bar 10)  ...............................................................................................................

(b) What steps does the composer take to ensure that the solo violin will come through the texture of the other strings in bars 1–2?

.....................................................................................................................................................

(c) Identify the chords marked * in bars 2, 3, 9 and 10 by writing on the dotted lines below. Use either words or symbols. State the position of each chord and whether it is major, minor, augmented or diminished. Treat them all as in the key of D major.

bar 2  ...................................................          bar 3 (vocal parts)  ...........................................

bar 9 (vocal parts)  ..............................          bar 10 (vocal parts)  .........................................

(d) Mark clearly on the score, using the appropriate capital letter for identification, one example of each of the following. Also give the bar numbers of your answers.

A   a harmonic interval of a major 7th sounding between two parts of the same string section.

Bar(s) ............

B   a 9–8 suspension in the string parts.   Bar(s) ............

C   a tonic chord with major 7th in the vocal parts.   Bar(s) ............

D   syncopation in the vocal parts.   Bar(s) ............

E   a plucked triple-stop.   Bar ............

(e) Describe briefly the effect and mood of the vocal writing, showing how the words of the text are reflected in the setting.

.....................................................................................................................................................

.....................................................................................................................................................

(f) Complete the following statements:

The vocal parts change chords and syllables together and this style of writing is called ......................,

whereas the string parts (e.g. bars 1–2) show writing which is more ........................... . An unusual

feature in bar 4 of the vocal parts for the male voices is the .............................................. . There is

imitation of bar 5 of the solo violin part an octave lower by the .............................. in bar ....... .

(g) Answer **TRUE** or **UNTRUE** to each of the following statements:

(i)   The only string section which is not divided somewhere is the double bass.   .........................

(ii)  The viola last note of bar 6 is the highest sound at that point.   .........................

(iii) None of the string parts changes clef.   .........................

(iv)  All of the notes for harp in bars 11–12 are doubled at the unison somewhere among the first and second violin parts.   .........................

5.     Study this extract and then answer the questions below.

(a)  Identify the chords marked * in bars 5, 6, 7 and 14 by writing on the dotted lines below. Use either
     words or symbols. State the position of each chord, whether it is major, minor, augmented or
     diminished, and the prevailing key for each chord.

     bar 5   ..........................................     key ....................................
     bar 6   ..........................................     key ....................................
     bar 7   ..........................................     key ....................................
     bar 14  ..........................................     key ....................................

(b)  Write out the parts for clarinets and horns in bars 7–8 as they would sound at concert pitch. Use
     the appropriate key signature.

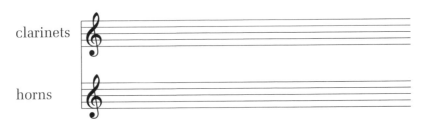

**(c)** Mark clearly on the score, using the appropriate capital letter for identification, one example of each of the following. Also give the bar numbers of your answers.

**A**    a bar with two appoggiaturas in a string part.    Bar ............

**B**    an unaccented chromatic passing note.    Bar ............

**C**    a falling interval of a diminished 5th in a string part.    Bar(s) ............

**D**    a chromatic lower auxiliary note.    Bar ............

**E**    a $^6_4$–$^5_3$ (Ic–V) progression.    Bar(s) ............

**F**    the harmonic interval of an augmented 4th sounding between two of the same wind instruments.    Bar(s) ............

**(d)** Complete the following statements:

The extract is made up of ................... phrases with the following bar numbers ..........................
........................................ . The non-harmony notes in bar 5 are .......... and ......................................
semiquavers of the second violin part. Apart from the clarinets and horns, the other instrument used here which does not sound at concert pitch is the .................................................. . It sounds
.................................................. than written.

**(e)** Write out the part for Violin I in bar 15 as you think it should be played.

**(f)** Which instruments from the standard string and woodwind sections of the orchestra are **not** required to play here?

| | | | |
|---|---|---|---|
| string | ................................................. | clef(s) used | ......................................... |
| woodwind | ................................................. | clef(s) used | ......................................... |
| | ................................................. | clef(s) used | ......................................... |
| | ................................................. | clef(s) used | ......................................... |

**(g)** Describe the mood of the music and the part played by the instruments and sections in achieving it.

..............................................................................................................................................................
..............................................................................................................................................................
..............................................................................................................................................................
..............................................................................................................................................................

**(h)** Underline the name of the likely composer from the list below:

         Handel       Debussy       Beethoven       Sibelius

Give the reasons for your choice.

..............................................................................................................................................................
..............................................................................................................................................................
..............................................................................................................................................................

6.  Study the opening from the Concerto Grosso printed opposite, and then answer the questions below. (The figures have been omitted from the bass throughout.)

(a) (i)  What do you understand by the term Ripieno?  ..................................................................

    (ii)  Describe the role played here by the Concertino and mention two features which show that the instrumental parts in it are more soloistic than those of the Ripieno.

          ................................................................................................................................................

          ................................................................................................................................................

(b) Mark clearly on the score, using the appropriate capital letter for identification, one example of each of the following **from the tutti parts of the extract**. Also give the bar numbers of your answers.

    A   a dominant 7th chord in third inversion in the key of G minor.   Bar(s) ............

    B   a dominant 7th chord in third inversion in the key of F major.   Bar(s) ............

    C   a major chord with 7th on the subdominant of G minor.   Bar(s) ............

    D   a second inversion of a major chord on the flattened supertonic of G minor (Neapolitan).

        Bar(s) ............

(c) Answer TRUE or UNTRUE to each of the following statements:

    (i)   The harmonic interval between the cello and second violin on the last beat of bar 12 is a compound minor 7th.   ........................

    (ii)  There is a 4–3 suspension in bar 11.   ........................

    (iii) The first violin part in both the Concertino and Ripieno in bars 1–9 is the same.   ......................

(d) Comment on the use and musical effect of (i) dynamic marks and (ii) pauses and rests in the section from bar 14 to the end of the extract.

    (i)   ...........................................................................................................................................

          ...........................................................................................................................................

    (ii)  ...........................................................................................................................................

          ...........................................................................................................................................

(e) Complete the following statements:

    The indications **Largo e affettuoso** at the start mean ................................................................ .

    There is a changing note in the first violin (Concertino) part in bar 3 and the note is ......... . There

    is a note of anticipation in the same part at an imperfect cadence in bar ....... and the note is ....... .

    There is an example of a hemiola in bars ................ .

(f) Make a list of the instruments which you think might be suitable for playing the part here for 'Basso e Continuo'.

    ................................................................................................................................................

(g) Underline the name of the likely composer from the list below:

                    Handel        Lassus        Rossini        Brahms

    Give the reasons for your choice. ........................................................................................

    ................................................................................................................................................

# Answers to Question 4

These are specimen answers. Alternative responses are often possible, and will receive credit if they accurately answer part of or the full requirements of the question.

1. **(a)**  **A**   bars 22–23       **B**   bar 39       **C**   bar 36

   **(b)**  bar 15                    *or*                    bar 27

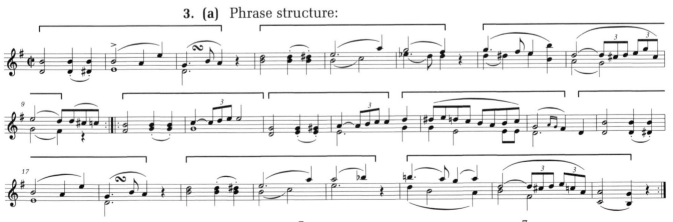

   **(c)**  bar 30: B and G♮       bar 31: F

   **(d)**  Similarities:  same rhythm and note patterns in first six bars of each;
   same cadential harmonies (bars 13–16 and bars 29–32)
   Differences:  key: bars 1–16 in A minor but bars 17–32 in C major
   melody: bars 7–8 different to bars 22–23 *or*
   bars 13–16 different to bars 29–32

   **(e)**  two or four;      8;      double suspension;      F major;      D minor

2. **(a)**  bar 3:   $V^7$c (major) in A major       bar 18:  iib (minor) in A major
   bar 19:  vii$^{\text{dim7}}$ (diminished) in F♯ minor
   bar 20:  vii°$^7$c (diminished) in A major

   **(b)**  **A**   bar 6, beats 1–2 *or* bar 7, beat 3
   **B**   bars 11–12       **C**   bar 23 *or* bar 24       **D**   bar 20

   **(c)**  it appears in the voice (and piano) in bars 2–3 and bars 12–13,
   and in the piano alone in bars 14–15;
   the same rhythm is used throughout bars 4–10 and bars 16–18 but
   with the final minim usually sub-divided into two crotchets;
   the voice alone uses the rhythm in bars 15–16;
   the inner parts of the piano part use the dotted rhythm in the two
   final bars, but it is here displaced to the first beat of the bar,
   losing the accentuation of the rhythm

   **(d)**  A major;      E major;      $V^7$;      A major;      D major;      B minor

   **(e)**  Mendelssohn (*Frage* Op. 9 No. 1)
   harmonic idiom too rich for Bach or Haydn, but insufficiently
   advanced for Alban Berg;
   concentration on melody, and detailed performing directions,
   characteristic of Romantic composers

3. **(a)**  Phrase structure:

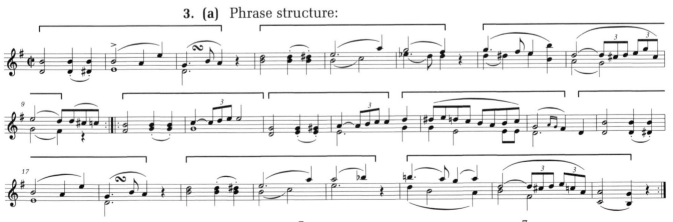

   **(b)**  bar 2:  $IV^7$ (major) in G major       bar 6:  $V^7$d (major) in G major
   bar 10:  $V^7$c (major) in C major       bar 12:  $V^7$c (major) in A minor
   bar 21:  ♯iv$^{\text{dim7}}$ (diminished) in G major

(c)     bar 3               *or*               bar 15               *or*

(d)  **A**     bar 14 (D♯)          **B**     C♯ in bar 23
     **C**     bar 2, beat 3 *or* bar 5, beat 3
     **D**     bar 18
     **E**     bar 2, beat 3 *or* bar 3, beat 2½ *or* bar 5, beat 4
     **F**     bar 14, beat 2 *or* bar 17, beat 2½ *or* bar 20, beat 1

(e)  E minor;     C major;     A minor;     imperfect;     G major

(f)  1.     bars 21–24 have a different melody to bars 6–9
     2.     bars 8–9 modulate to D, bars 23–24 end in tonic (G)

(g)  Schubert (Adagio in G, D.178)
     harmonic style too chromatic for Handel or Haydn, but
     characteristic of Schubert (especially cadences); piano figuration
     not typical of Chopin; the song-like melody with chordal
     accompaniment is a feature of Schubert's music, as is the frequent
     use of the ♩ ♪♪ ♩ rhythm

4.  (a)  bar 3:   ii⁷ (minor) in D major          bar 5:   V⁷b (major) in A major
         bar 14:  vii° (diminished) in D major

    (b)  **A**     bar 7, beat 1 to bar 8, beat 2 *or* bar 13, beat 1 to bar 14, beat 2
         **B**     bar 1 (first G) *or* bar 3 (second F♯) *or* bar 9 (penultimate A)
         **C**     bar 3, beat 1 *or* bar 8, first A          **D**     bar 8, last C♯
         **E**     bar 12 (G to E♯)          **F**     bar 14 (E to F♯)
         **G**     bar 2, D♯ *or* bar 6, last D♯          **H**     bar 13, beats 3–4

    (c)  C♯;     A;     F♯;     third D

    (d)  bar 11:   compound minor 6th
         bar 14:   minor 10th *or* compound minor 3rd

    (e)  three three-bar phrases, separated by the rests in bars 3 and 6
         (some sub-division of these phrases is possible)

    (f)  A major;     imperfect;     pedal;     suspensions *or* sequences

    (g)  bar 1, beats 1–2          bar 11, beat 3          bar 15, beat 2

    (h)  Similarity:     same musical material
         Difference:     transposed down a 5th to end in the tonic

5.  (a)  **A**     bar 2          **B**     bar 19, beat 2          **C**     bars 7–8

    (b)  (i)     1.     bars 5–6 (clarinet)     2.     bars 6–7 (piano, right hand)
                 3.     bars 13–14 (clarinet)
         (ii)    same rhythm
         (iii)   bars 19–20

    (c)

    (d)  bar 1:     i♭⁷d (minor)          bar 3:     iv⁷ (minor)
         bar 4:     V⁷d (major)          bar 7:     VI⁷ (major)
         bar 12:    vii^dim7 (diminished)  bar 14:    IV^♯3b (major)

    (e)  1.     use of crescendo and/or the direction *pesante* (heavily)
         2.     ever decreasing note values culminating in trills on
                the dominant
         3.     descending chromatic octaves over a dominant pedal

    (f)  (i)     UNTRUE          (ii)     TRUE          (iii)     TRUE

**6. (a)** phrases two and four are only three bars long

  **(b)** left-hand;  falling third;  two parts;  a little quicker;
  syncopated *or* offbeat;  last;  right-hand;  octave

  **(c)** bars 25–26 *or* bars 28–30

  **(d)** canon;  bar;  octave;  opening theme;
  major;  quick;  light;  one string (*una corda*)

  **(e)** it is harmonised (using an inner (inverted) dominant pedal in the
  first two phrases); first phrase is repeated an octave higher;
  final C of first phrase replaced by E♮; last phrase extended to four
  bars and uses mainly just the implied harmony of this part of the
  theme

  **(f)** bars 69–70 *or* bars 73–74

  **(g)** walking pace;  F minor;  heavy;  half;  first;  perfect;  very quiet

  **(h) A**  G in bar 87 *or* bar 91  **B**  bar 91, beat 2

  **(i)** VI (major);  III (major);  ii°b (diminished);  $i^{\flat 7}$d (minor)

# Answers to Question 5

These are specimen answers. Alternative responses are often possible, and
will receive credit if they accurately answer part of or the full requirements
of the question.

**1. (a)** piccolo;  4 timpani (kettle drums);  viola

  **(b) (i)**  clarinets

    bassoons

    horns in F

    horns in D

    **(ii)** 1.  piccolo; octave higher  2.  double bass; octave lower

  **(c) A**  any sharpened offbeat quaver in bars 5–6 *or* 13–16
    **B**  bars 5–6 *or* 13–14 (horns) *or* 15–16 (horns or trumpets)
    **C**  bars 18–19, viola

  **(d) (i)** timpani; 9–12  **(ii)** $\frac{3}{2}$  **(iii)** 18

**2. (a)** bass drum;  timpani;  moderate waltz speed/tempo;
  first player;  held very long, always getting quieter;  hand stopped

  **(b)** clarinets, bars 39–40

    I. II

  horns, bars 21–27

    III. IV

  **(c) (i)**

  **(ii)** one

**(d) A**    bars 26–27 (horns III and IV)
   **B**    bar 40 (violins 1 and 2)
   **C**    bar 18 (viola)    **D**    bar 22, beat 1 (solo violin)

**(e)** diminuendo;    $\boldsymbol{f}$;    $\boldsymbol{pp}$;    bar 12 *or* bar 13;    beat *or* note;
   static;    $^6_4$ (ic);    dominant;    (repeated) semiquavers

**(f)** 5;    octave;    second violins;    first violins;    octave;
   crotchet;    augmentation;    imitated

**(g)** trumpets; trombones; (tuba)    triangle; cymbals, etc.

**3. (a)** a little slower than walking pace (it can also mean a little quicker);
   divided, plucked;    both players play the same notes

**(b) (i)**

**(ii)**

**(c)** G major;    ii (minor);    $V^7$ (major);    I (major) ;    $^\sharp iv^{dim7}c$ (diminished)

**(d) A**    bar 4 *or* bar 14 (cor anglais) *or* bar 9 *or* bar 19 (flute)
   **B**    bar 18 (first bassoon)    **C**    bar 13 *or* bar 18 (violin I)
   **D**    bar 6 (the note A) *or* bar 16 (the note B) *or* similar places

**(e) (i)** oboe    **(ii)** through a double reed    **(iii)** treble

**(f)** small orchestra;    low dynamic levels;    gentle pace;
   repetitive triplet rhythms;    repetitive melodies;
   simple 'tune and accompaniment' texture;    simple harmony;
   double reed instrument often associated with folk music

**4. (a)** sustained;    always with mute;    play in the ordinary (usual) way;
   all play the same notes (after a divided section)

**(b)** high pitch;    unmuted (accompanying strings are muted);
   enters first, catching the attention;    lower strings silent

**(c)** $I^{(7)}c$ (major);    $ii^7b$ (minor) *or* $IV^6$ (major);
   $IV^{\flat 7}$ (major);    $ii^7d$ (minor) *or* $IVc^6$ (major)

**(d) A**    bar 5 (viola, B–A$\sharp$)    **B**    bar 6 (violins, F$\sharp$)
   **C**    bar 8, beat 1 *or* bar 10, beat 1 (bar 3, beat 2, has a passing 7th)
   **D**    bar 4 ('and the')    **E**    bar 3 *or* bar 4 (cello)

**(e)** the low dynamic, slow pace, mainly static rhythm, legato phrasing
   and homophonic vocal texture all contribute to a 'soft stillness';
   the mystery of the 'night' is highlighted by a surprising shift to
   B major; 'sweet harmony' is provided by added 6ths and 7ths and
   thick vocal textures; the word 'sweet' is coloured by an
   unprepared and unresolved flat 7th

**(f)** homophonic;    contrapuntal (or polyphonic);
   low note (bottom D) for basses;    first violins;    6

**(g) (i)** TRUE    **(ii)** UNTRUE    **(iii)** UNTRUE    **(iv)** UNTRUE

**5. (a)** bar 5:    $V^7b$ (major); E$\flat$ major
   bar 6:    $V^7b$ (major); F minor
   bar 7:    vii$^{\circ 7}$ (diminished); B$\flat$ major
   bar 14:    $ii^7b$ (minor); E$\flat$ major

**(b)**

**(c)**    **A**    bar 7       **B**    bar 12       **C**    bar 7 (cello/bass)
      **D**    bar 5 (F♯) *or* bar 8 *or* bar 10 (A♮)     **E**    bar 8
      **F**    bar 2 *or* bar 3 *or* bar 15 (clarinets)

**(d)**   three *or* four;     1–8, 9–12 (or 9–10, 11–12), 13–16
                   *or* four phrases of four bars each;
      F♯;      the third G;     double bass;     an octave lower

**(e)**                           *(other versions possible)*

**(f)**   string:       viola, alto C clef (and treble clef)
      woodwind:   flute, treble clef; oboe, treble clef;
                    bassoon, bass and tenor (occasionally treble) clefs

**(g)**   a fast speed, short note values and major key make the music
lively, buoyant and cheerful; a light accompaniment of mainly
detached notes supports a more legato melody which is on first
violins throughout; loud tutti chords emphasise dominant 7th
harmony in the second half, where the melody becomes even
more active, before the opening mood returns after the pause

**(h)**   Beethoven (Contradance in E flat)
instruments used and the melodic/harmonic style preclude Handel;
too simple in orchestration, texture and harmony for Debussy or
Sibelius; the dynamic contrasts, functional harmony and regular
phrasing are all typical of Beethoven

**6. (a) (i)**   the main body of the orchestra (literally 'full')
       **(ii)**   they play the same music as the Ripieno, but in only three
parts; they also have solo passages; these include multiple
stops and higher parts (e.g. cello in tenor clef)

**(b)**   **A**   bar 5    **B**   bar 20    **C**   bar 19    **D**   bar 16, beat 2

**(c)**   **(i)**   UNTRUE    **(ii)**   TRUE    **(iii)**   TRUE

**(d) (i)**   there are sudden and dramatic changes of dynamic: loud at
bar 14 with the ripieno entry, suddenly quiet for the Neapolitan
chord in bar 16, loud for the interrupted cadence in bar 19 and
very quiet for the final concertino passage
       **(ii)**   a short but dramatic rest announces the unexpected chord in
bar 19, which is prolonged with a pause; rests come before
the final tutti and concertino entries in order to maintain the
structure of phrases which start on the second beat of the bar

**(e)**   slow and tenderly;    D;      8;      D;      17–18

**(f)**   cello, double bass (possibly bassoon), harpsichord, organ, lute

**(g)**   Handel (Concerto Grosso No. 6 in G minor)
Lassus wrote in a stricter and usually more polyphonic style for
voices; both Rossini and Brahms used a more complex harmonic
idiom; the terraced dynamics (devoid of cresc. and dim. markings)
and contrasts in texture, as well as the use of basso continuo, are
all hallmarks of the early 18th century; Handel wrote many
Concerti Grossi, while the other composers wrote no works in this
genre